A CHIL
THE THIRTIES

A CHILD OF THE THIRTIES

KEN HANKINS

JANUS PUBLISHING COMPANY
London, England

First published in Great Britain 1999
by Janus Publishing Company Limited,
Edinburgh House, 19 Nassau Street,
London W1N 7RE

www.januspublishing.co.uk

A CIP catalogue record for this book
is available from the British Library.

ISBN 1 85756 406 5

Phototypeset in 11 on 14 Sabon
by Keyboard Services, Luton, Beds

Cover design John Anastasio, Creative Line

Printed and bound in Great Britain by
Athenaeum Press Ltd, Gateshead, Tyne & Wear

DEDICATION

This book is dedicated with love to Rachel,
the author's granddaughter.

CONTENTS

ACKNOWLEDGEMENTS

An acknowledgement of thanks in helping to prepare this book for publication to Peter Bennett, friend and colleague of the author.

A CHILD OF THE THIRTIES

IT WAS AN AGE of innocence. It was an age when the majority of the poor lived in blessed ignorance of what could and should have been, without envy of those better placed and stoically accepting their lot as though God had written to them personally, officially confirming that that was the way it had to be.

It was an age of honesty, a time when most schoolboys thought that the most criminal act they could commit was to ride their bicycles on the pavement or without lights after dark, and their parents considered that inability to pay a small debt at the corner shop was only a couple of degrees less shameful than having a murderer in the family.

It was an age of genuine poverty, when an empty purse or an empty wallet certainly meant empty stomachs for those unable to obtain credit or unwilling to experience the indignity of asking for it.

It was, of course, Great Britain of the Thirties, a pathetically conducted decade, riddled with grossly unfair contrasts, disgraceful exploitation and monumental indifference to the predicament of the under-privileged.

Schoolchildren were subjected to hours of geography and history lessons, the former joyfully ramming home the fact that Britain had a benign influence over at least a quarter of the globe and its inhabitants, and the latter subject, no less joyfully, setting out in jingoistic detail the wars and conquests that had brought about this apparent domination of the world stage.

Yet few, if any, of these pupils ever asked themselves the question: if this country is so rich, so powerful, so influential, why do we have bread and dripping for dinner sometimes, instead of a hot, nourishing meal?

Such a poser troubled their parents even less. After all, most of the national newspapers told them repeatedly that there was no country to match this one – and the trusting readers dutifully believed it.

Money was always in short supply for the poor. Admittedly, sixpence would buy anything on the counters at Woolworth's, a reasonable suit could be purchased for 50 shillings, and there would be change out of half-a-crown after selecting a modest joint of beef at the Co-op butcher's shop.

But measured against a weekly income below £3 for the average working-class family, such items were not regarded as cheap, especially by those breadwinners who had four or five to feed and clothe.

The majority of families got by, of course, but at a price. Labourers in the pits, quarries and furnaces grew old and bent before their time, factory workers in unhealthy environments inherited industrial diseases that cut them down as if by a scythe, and many of the aged finished their days in state hospital institutions that, for all the efforts of the nursing staff, were bleak and cheerless places that undermined the will to live.

Many died young, afflicted with the scourge of consumption. There were all sorts of epidemics practically every year – scarlet fever, smallpox, chickenpox, measles and, most feared of all, infantile paralysis. The toll was relentless.

Those who survived these perils grew tough and wiry, brushing aside minor ills with spartan fortitude. This ability at an early age to absorb everything that life could throw at them held them in good stead in the painful growing-up years and, more importantly, in the war that came upon the world as the decade drew to a close.

Working men found solace in a pint or two at the club or pub and a packet of cigarettes from the corner shop. Their families did not grudge them these little luxuries. They were small comforts for the men who strove to maintain their wives and children in an era that appeared to offer no prospect of improvement.

Yet for all the harshness, the years of the Thirties often provided magical times for the young. There were many bitter moments but there were sweet ones, too, with much laughter to be heard and simple fun to be had.

Corporal punishment was handed out both in the school and in the home but, for all that, children were loved and cherished. They were safe from real harm in the community, being able to play in the dark streets at night without fear of molestation, abduction or worse. It was as if the fates knew they had enough to cope with in life without having to face extra dangers from their own kind. The children of the Thirties may have been poor in the material sense, but they were rich in other ways, although they may not have recognised it then.

The stories that follow are built around a boy's adventures in a typical Midlands boot- and shoe-producing town of the period. They all happened more than half a century ago, but the memories of them are so strong they could have happened yesterday.

FIVE AUNTS AND A JOINT BIRTHDAY PRESENT

TO BE FATHERLESS in the Thirties was an unenviable experience for any child, but was especially so if your mother did not have a home of her own and had to support you and herself on the 35 shillings a week she earned for $5^1/_2$ days of labour in a boot and shoe factory.

Home to me, over a lean span of six years, happened to be the house of whichever relative felt disposed to allow us the use of a spare bedroom for a few weeks or months. We shunted around from one to another as the spirit of hospitality waned and the current hosts felt that it was time for another member of the family to undertake some responsibility for their itinerant kith and kin.

My father, an amiable barber with a fondness for backing racehorses, died when I was three, leaving my mother with an uphill struggle for survival that continued even after she married for a second time.

Some of the fatherless of those times gained succour from aunts they could turn to when life became even harder and prospects even dimmer. I was blessed – or cursed – with five such ladies. Their names were Nell, Elsie, Flo, Kate and Maud. They were big and buxom women and they all looked like a picture of the music-hall artiste, Florrie Forde, that I had seen on the front of a piece of sheet music.

Over the years they brought me joy and unhappiness in just

about equal proportions. It all depended on their individual moods and the state of relationships within a family that seemed constantly in the throes of civil war. The trouble was that they were, without exception, tough and uncompromising women – far more aggressive and assertive than their generally gentle, mild-mannered husbands.

This female dominance was surprising, bearing in mind that all five husbands had served in the trenches in the Great War and had taken part in appalling battles. Perhaps that was why they were so compliant and willing to let their spouses take the lead in everything. Perhaps they felt that even a minor domestic squabble was not worth becoming involved in after all they had been through in Flanders.

Strangely enough, despite their constant quarrels, the five sisters could not bear being without each other's company for long, and on most Saturday and Sunday nights they used to assemble at the local trades and labour club, dutifully accompanied by their husbands.

They always sat at the same wrought-iron table in the large bar. Over the years the other members of the club had come to accept that this particular table was unofficially reserved for the Big Five and no one had the temerity to try to take over their territory.

And so they sat all evening, the ladies sipping their stouts and ports and lemon, the men swallowing their pints of mild and bitter, carefully timing the emptying of their glasses to coincide with each other so it did not look as though they were trying to force the hand of the one whose turn it was to buy the next round.

Sometimes the evenings passed without incident, the steady flow of drinks encouraging a mood of conviviality among the sisters. But sometimes those self-same drinks led to indiscreet or ill-chosen words of personal criticism, which, in turn, led to harsh exchanges and a swift break-up of the party.

It would need only one small piece of fault-finding to split the sisters into two warring factions, for it was a well-established understanding that when two of them fell out, the other three had to take sides in the dispute. There was no such thing as neutrality. Consequently, it could be three against two or four against one. Doubtless they found it a refreshing change from the times when they were all in agreement and the five of them presented a formidable front against the rest of the world.

These bar rows, always verbal, never physical, invariably started in the most innocuous fashion. For example, Aunt Maud might say to Aunt Kate, 'I don't think that new hat of yours goes with your coat.'

The five husbands would look at each other uneasily. These battle-hardened veterans of much inter-family strife could recognise trouble a mile off. They would stay silent and wait for the explosion.

Aunt Kate's mouth, always a tight, thin line, would tighten even further. There would be much meaningful sniffing and the gripping of fingers around handbags on laps as the other three sisters awaited Kate's answer to this insult to her sartorial tastes. Whose side they took in the dispute would depend to a large extent on Kate's reply and the manner of its delivery.

Her icy retort would not be long in coming. It might be something like, 'It's better than going out in a blouse that wants a good wash.'

Maud, who may already have forgotten that she had made the remark that had put the match to the powder keg, would turn to her husband, sitting nervously at her side.

'Did you hear that, Jack? Did you hear what she just said?' Jack, who was wise as well as easy-going, would pretend he had not heard the questions. He would, perhaps, duck his head under the table and go through the motions of looking for a lost coin.

Seeing that she would not be getting any support from this

direction, Maud would launch her verbal retaliation, recalling old failings, errors of judgment and past squabbles that everyone thought had been forgiven and forgotten.

Kate would defend herself stoutly in similar style and, having decided whose side they should be on, Nell, Elsie and Flo would enter the lists. It would all be very noisy, providing everyone in the bar with a welcome cabaret act. Club members would sit entranced and would be disappointed when the verbal ructions came to an end.

The conclusion of these family rows usually came when one of the protagonists ran out of unkind things to say. Rather than remain mute and take more punishment like a beaten boxer trapped on the ropes, she would say, 'I'm not standing for any more of this, Jack. Take me home.'

And off she would go, marching out with as much dignity as she could muster, closely followed by Jack, who would look at the floor to avoid eye contact with the amused watchers. The remaining sisters and their embarrassed spouses would empty their glasses at top speed and set off in crocodile fashion for the exit door.

As far as the club members were concerned, the entertainment was over for the evening, the end of a fleeting diversion that made a rollicking change from the more serious matters of working-class life.

The five sisters, on the other hand, knew that there would be a couple of weeks of animosity and ill-feeling within the group, involving much backbiting and many recriminations, before a peace treaty could be signed and they could come together again for another nice family party at the trades and labour club.

Such was the awesome reputation of these five aunts that when they called a family meeting at my grandmother's council house, my mother and I feared the worst. As far as I was concerned, the events that followed confirmed my fears.

The summit conference took place a few weeks before my ninth birthday and it was this forthcoming minor event in the family calendar that had prompted the gathering of the clan.

The aunts sat in a circle in granny's sparsely furnished living-room. Their husbands perched on the well-scrubbed dining-table or propped themselves against the wall. They all puffed away at Woodbine cigarettes with a dedication to the task that verged on the fanatical.

It might be useful to establish who was married to whom in this oddly assorted tribe. The five husbands may have been united in a common desire for peace, quiet and freedom from any sort of confrontation, but apart from that they were as unalike as chalk and cheese, both physically and temperamentally.

Uncle Walt was married to Aunt Nell. He was a big, bluff man with a balding head and a 'hail fellow, well met' attitude to all and sundry that made me, even as a youngster, sometimes doubt his sincerity. However, he had two personal possessions that put him above the rest as far as I was concerned – a bone-handled knife and a fork that legend said he had taken from the blood-stained tunic of a German machine-gunner he had bayoneted to death in a trench on the Somme.

I used to love visiting Aunt Nell's house at meal times just so that I could see him cutting up his meat with his much-prized spoils of war. Every time he lifted the fork to his mouth I could picture the dramatic fight in the mud and imagine the shouts and screams of the killers and those they were killing.

Uncle Ted was married to Aunt Elsie. He was a far different proposition: short, heavily built and possessing two of the most magnificent cauliflower ears I had ever seen. I never did discover how he came by these disfigurements. I asked often enough, but no one would tell me. I assumed he received them while boxing in his younger days but had early come to the conclusion that he could not have been a very good pugilist if he allowed his ears to suffer blows that turned them as shapeless as that. Uncle Ted said little, and when he did he spoke very fast, as though anxious to get the ordeal of talking over as soon as possible.

Uncle Bill was married to Aunt Flo. He was a dark man with a blue chin that was in constant need of a razor. He had a rasping voice, the result of being gassed during the war, and he swore a lot, although there was never any venom in his cursing.

He also had rapidly failing eyesight, which was particularly unfortunate as he was a bus driver. I remember at least two occasions when the double-decker vehicle he was steering bumped into walls on tight corners. He compensated for his eye weakness by driving his bus more slowly and carefully than his colleagues and consequently seldom kept to the timetables laid down. Happily for him, the bus company management never rumbled him and he got away with it for years – as did the unknowing motorists and cyclists who had to share the road with him.

Uncle Harry was married to Aunt Kate. He was the quiet man of the five, perhaps because he was a few years older than the others and had learned the wisdom of keeping his own counsel. He had an almost permanent smile, a little facial mannerism that turned up the corners of his mouth a fraction and gave him, surprisingly, a rather cunning look. I always thought Uncle Harry knew more than he ever let on.

Uncle Jack was married to Aunt Maud. He was tall and slim and something of a dandy. His detachable collars were always snowy white and his trousers were never without a crease. I suspect that he liked the ladies, but fear of retribution from Aunt Maud kept him on the straight and narrow.

They formed an impressive group of ten and my mother looked apprehensive as she stood in front of the fire and waited to learn the reason for the mass visitation. It was all too much for me. I went into the kitchen and tried to listen through the door.

Aunt Elsie, most forthright of all the sisters, made the announcement. 'We've come about Ronnie's birthday,' she said.

My heart gave a jump. There must be something special in the wind if they were all prepared to turn out on a dingy Sunday afternoon in order to reveal plans for my anniversary.

'We are not going to waste money on buying toys or books for him this year,' she continued. 'We are going to put it to better use.'

My heart, which was working overtime, did not jump at this revelation. It sank. I did not really want to know any more but I had to find out what dreadful scheme they had up their collective sleeve.

'We've decided on a joint birthday present,' said Aunt Elsie, in a positive tone that left no room for modification. 'We are going to kit him out.'

For a moment I thought she had said 'kick him out', but then it dawned on me that she was using one of Uncle Ted's army expressions.

My mother said nothing, having discovered long ago in childhood, as the youngest in the family, that there was little point in arguing with any of her sisters once they had made up their minds.

'Flo and Bill are going to buy him a nice overcoat they have seen in the Co-op,' said Elsie. 'Maud and Jack will get him a new cap and some socks. Kate and Harry have seen a smart pair of trousers and a tie, and Ted and me are thinking of a shirt and some gloves.'

Aunt Nell butted in. 'And my Walt's going to make him a pair of boots,' she said proudly.

All members of the family recognised that Uncle Walt was a true craftsman of the boot and shoe industry. Like some of his

11

contemporaries, he could make items of footwear from start to finish, taking in every part of the complicated process.

'A hand-made pair of boots,' said Aunt Nell, pushing the fact home to make sure my mother did not underestimate the value of the gift. 'They'll last Ronnie for years. They'll never wear out, will they, Walt?'

Uncle Walt voiced his agreement. It was a well-known fact that when he made footwear of any sort it was intended to last – and it did.

By this time I had opened the kitchen door and stood watching the family scene. I knew I was plumbing the depths of ingratitude, but it was one of those moments when I almost wished I had been an orphan.

Uncle Walt reached inside his coat and pulled out a square piece of cardboard. He placed it on the table.

'Take your shoes off, Ronnie, and get up on here,' he said.

I clambered onto the table and he told me to place my left foot on the cardboard. He then took a pencil from his waistcoat pocket and drew round the outline of my foot.

'Now the other one,' he said, turning over the cardboard. My right foot was duly outlined.

With that, the clan departed, assuring my mother once again that, come my birthday, I would be the best-dressed kid in the street, if not the town. I awaited the arrival of these well-intentioned gifts with little or no enthusiasm.

On the morning of my birthday – a Saturday – my mother produced the combined family presents from a cupboard where they had been hidden from prying eyes. She watched as I slowly and reluctantly put on the clothes – shirt, socks, trousers, overcoat, gloves, boots and, finally, the cap.

'Let's have a good look at you,' she said. I stood to attention with my arms tightly by my sides, struggling against an urge to burst into tears.

There was no doubting the quality of the clothes, but there

was something terribly wrong. None of them fitted. Not only were they too big, they were *far* too big. The size of everything practically suffocated me.

The trousers reached down to the top of my socks and the overcoat fell only a few inches short of my ankles. The shirt collar was almost large enough to accommodate another neck and the gloves were of such proportions that it would be impossible to pick up anything while wearing them.

As for the cap, it came close to defying description. It was as big as a dinner plate, with a massive peak that jutted out several inches. To crown it all, it had a decorative button on top that looked like a gobstopper.

Worst of all were the boots. They were big enough and stout enough for mountain climbing or kicking down doors. They were at least three sizes more than they should have been, and even with the laces pulled tight there was still an appreciable gap between my thin ankles and the unyielding leather. The bulbous toecaps were as hard as rocks and there were large metal tips on the heels and toes of the soles. True to his promise, Uncle Walt had made them to last.

My mother made no comment, but I noticed that her face had a sad look and her eyes were watery. I knew that she felt for me at that moment, but there were no words of comfort. Instead, she reminded me that it was time we set off on a grand tour of all the aunts and uncles so that they could see me attired in my new outfit.

From my point of view it was a depressing outing; from their point of view my appearance was the realisation of a master plan. They were well aware, of course, that not a single article of the clothing fitted properly, but that, after all, had been the idea in the first place.

Without exception, every aunt said, 'We bought them big so that he could grow into them.'

We were treated to a cup of tea here, a biscuit or two there, but these welcome refreshments did little to lift my melancholy. I was too busy picturing a lifetime within the confines of those wretched clothes – much as a convict would contemplate an endless stretch behind bars.

I hated every item in this joint birthday present but I hated two of them far above the others – the monster cap and the giant boots.

I had hoped that my mother would walk back to my granny's house, where we were temporarily in residence, without passing along Edmund Street. If there was one area of the town to be avoided by a small boy it was Edmund Street – especially if he was clad in the way I happened to be.

The reason? It was the happy hunting ground of Maxie York and his gang, a villainous bunch, who, even at the tender ages of nine or ten, seemed hell-bent on getting to borstal by the quickest possible route.

They would lurk in doorways and alleyways, watching out for unwary travellers, particularly those foolhardy enough to try to walk down Edmund Street on their own. Having cornered their victim, Maxie and the boys would set about him with a ruthless disregard for the Queensberry Rules, or any other rules for that matter.

They also had a nice line in verbal abuse. This was reserved for those boys they considered too big to tackle physically. And the insults were always shouted from the other side of the road, thus giving them a flying start when the time came to make a run for it.

For some unknown reason, as we turned into Edmund Street my mother took hold of my hand. I was horrified. If Maxie and his boys saw me hand-in-hand with my mother my reputation at school, such as it was, would be in tatters.

My hopes of avoiding a confrontation were unfulfilled. The fates must have had it in for me that day, for Maxie and his wrecking crew were watching and waiting.

As we drew nearer and they were able to take in the full nature of my apparel, they shrieked with laughter, pointing their fingers and stamping their feet.

'Look, he's got his dad's boots on,' howled Maxie.

I stopped and tried to turn back, but my mother took a firmer grip on my hand and pulled me along.

'Take no notice,' she said. 'They are only jealous.'

For the life of me I could not see what they had to be jealous about. It would be akin to being envious of someone suffering with toothache.

Having unleashed one well-received witticism, Maxie produced another to entertain his friends. 'Go and fetch seven pounds of potatoes in your cap!' he shouted.

That was too much for me, even in my demoralised state. I wrenched myself free from my mother's grasp and tried to set off across the street to challenge my tormentors. My mother was too quick for me. She grabbed me by the shoulders, clipped my ear, and, pushing me ahead of her as though rolling a boulder up a hill, continued the journey along Edmund Street.

The spectacle filled Maxie and his gang with delight and they trailed along behind us, chanting, 'He's windy, he's windy!' – a schoolboy term meaning cowardice in the face of the enemy.

My humiliation was complete.

I dreaded the following day. It was Sunday, which meant Sunday School and the wearing of 'Sunday best'. Up until this moment I had never had a 'Sunday best', but now I had – in the shapeless form of the family's combined birthday present.

I knew that my mother would insist that I wore every item and I knew that meant more merciless ragging if the Edmund Street gang set eyes on me on my way to and from the school building.

As it turned out, getting to Sunday School was not too much

of a problem. It meant that I had to add to the length of my walk by taking detours along side streets. I also made a point of peeping round corners to see if Maxie and his cronies were on the loose and away from their native habitat.

I did not have to worry about meeting them at Sunday School. Maxie and company believed that only cissies went to Sunday School and their parents did little to persuade them otherwise.

Once I arrived at the stiflingly warm church room that housed our class, I was able to take off the heavy overcoat and stuff the equally outsize cap and gloves in the pockets. I felt almost human again.

All through the lengthy religious instruction, the prayers and the hymn singing, I allowed my mind to wander. I pondered on my tactics for getting home without an encounter with the awful Maxie. It was then, when I should have been concentrating on matters affecting my spiritual welfare, that I came up with an idea that just might add to my immediate temporal comfort and wellbeing.

I suddenly remembered the fate that had befallen a boy from a private school who had been unlucky enough to ride his bicycle along Edmund Street while wearing his school uniform. Memories of that incident raised my hopes to such an extent that I was able to put my worries behind me and concentrate on the Scripture lesson.

That, too, put my mind at rest, for, like my fellow pupils, I lived in fear of the wrath of the Lord – an attitude that sprang directly from the teachings of Miss Windrow, who ran the Sunday School.

She was a sharp-faced, unsmiling woman, thin as a rake and as pale as whitewash. She taught us to fear God as opposed to loving him, leaving the impressionable boys and girls in her class with the sure feeling that even the slightest misbehaviour brought the risk of instant punishment from on high. We did not know what form this retribution would take, but I suspected that it might be a thunderbolt that would roar through the heavens and strike me down where I stood.

Jesus, on the other hand, held no such fears for us. We were warmed by the pictures of him that hung on all four walls of the church room. His gentle face, sad eyes and noble bearing, even when being persecuted by his enemies, impressed us. We felt that we could trust him and he would see that we came to no real harm, whatever we did to offend him. All this was contrary to the fire and brimstone threats of the terrifying Miss Windrow.

The class concluded, I pulled on my overcoat, drew my cap low over my eyes and set off home. But there would be no dodging the perils of Edmund Street on this journey.

I marched along Sackville Street and turned left into Edmund Street. Dusk was on its way but it was still light enough for me to see Maxie and two of his pals hovering around one of the entries placed at intervals among the terraced houses.

Maxie spotted me immediately and was plainly ready to give chase as soon as I turned tail and ran. But I just kept walking towards them, almost as though they did not exist. Maxie and the gang could not believe their luck. It was like manna from heaven. They waited with ill-concealed excitement until I drew level and then the three of them began to circle round me like mongrel terriers tormenting a sheep in a field.

I stood stock still, with my arms by my sides, as Bobby and Des capered about in front of me and Maxie sneaked behind, ready for the pounce I hoped and prayed would come.

Then Maxie did it. He leapt forward and snatched the cap from my head and waved it around in triumph. This was followed by a little jig as he teasingly held out the cap, daring me to try to take it back.

'What you goin' to do about it, what you goin' to do about it?' he jeered, a chant taken up by his equally delighted lieutenants.

17

I remained still and silent. Maxie, his little blackcurrant eyes dancing and his cheeks red with pleasure, had known all along what he intended to do, but my refusal to attempt any form of defence led him to shorten the torture and get on with the deed. He turned away from me, gripped the cap by its peak and hurled it skywards in the direction of the sloping roofs. The cap flew off like a boomerang but, unlike a boomerang, it did not come back. It struck the side of a chimney and slid down the roof, ending in the guttering. All that could be seen of it now was about an inch and a half of the monstrous peak.

Maxie and the boys roared with laughter, pointing up at the roof and then putting their thumbs to their noses and waggling their fingers.

'Well, what you goin' to do *now*?' howled Maxie, flushed with achievement and wallowing in the admiration of his henchmen.

'Nothing,' I replied. I turned and walked away, deliberately scraping the steel tips of my heels on the pavement so that the sparks flew brightly in the fading light.

I had my back to them, so Maxie and his two friends could not see that I was smiling the broadest of smiles. I was a happy lad at that moment, but already my mind was wrestling with the next big problem in my young life: How could I get rid of those bloody boots?

THE FOUR-EYED
PRIZEFIGHTER

ONE OF THE MOST pleasurable activities for an enterprising working-class youngster in the Thirties was the collection of cigarette cards. One of the most unpleasant experiences was a trip to the school's clinic to have 'drops' in the eyes, administered by the strangely terrifying Nurse Craven.

These two emotional extremes came together for me one cold, hard winter during that unsparing decade. The connection was only a loose one but it led to a painful incident and a chain of events that left me a sadder if but wiser lad.

It was an odd adventure, linking as it did a bout of measles, an unwanted pair of spectacles, a short-lived but bloody street fight, the search for an elusive cigarette card, and a well-planned confidence trick.

You had to be poor, imaginative and a true seeker after knowledge to appreciate fully the joy of owning cigarette cards.

To begin with, most boys from hard-up families used cigarette cards – or 'photes', as they were popularly known – as currency. Pocket money was not easy to come by, so the cards took the place of coins.

For example, a quick dip into someone's bag of acid drops might cost two cards, a ten-minute read of a pal's comic could be anything up to 15 cards and a share of a bottle of lemonade on a hot day could result in an outlay of 25 cards. The 'price' at all times was dictated by the current state of the schoolboy financial market.

From this it can be seen that a boy with his pockets bulging with cigarette cards was rich indeed and never short of friends.

But it did not end there, for the avid card enthusiast liked to collect sets of cards – famous footballers and cricketers, stars of the silver screen and the wireless, breeds of dogs and wild birds of Great Britain. The cards were usually issued in sets of 50 and there was always a scramble to try to complete a series before a new one was issued by the crafty tobacco companies.

This resulted in gangs of eager boys hanging about outside tobacconists' shops, waiting for men to emerge with their packets of Woodbines, Gold Flake and Capstan Full Strength. As soon as a customer appeared, the cry would go up: 'Got any fag cards, mister?'

Depending on whether or not he had children of his own, the smoker would remove the card from the packet and hand it to whichever youngster he considered the most deserving. Sometimes, if we were lucky, the man would draw two or three more cards from the top pocket of his jacket and distribute them among us.

Apart from their currency value, and satisfying the collecting mania of those of us who liked to accumulate sets and stick them in albums supplied by the tobacco firms, these cards had an educational use. The reverse sides contained a wealth of information about the people and events shown on the fronts. Consequently, we supplemented our school learning by soaking up all sorts of facts and figures, ranging from the eating habits of gorillas to the length of the reign of King Richard II. Without doubt, the cigarette card played a big part in our formative years.

At the time of the adventure I am about to relate, I had

reached the final stage of a bid to complete the collection of a set of cards entitled 'Famous Cricketers'.

It had been an uphill struggle, but I had managed to pull together 49 of the set of 50, the only one missing being the Australian batsman and captain, Bill Woodfull. He was proving to be a difficult man to track down. No one seemed to have a spare of this noted sporting personality and those who had a copy could not be coaxed into parting with it, no matter how tempting I made the swap offer.

It was at this crucial point in my hunt that I was struck down with measles, an unpleasant and dangerous ailment in those days.

In addition to enduring the spots and fighting an almost irresistible desire to scratch them, the sufferer, on doctor's orders, had to lie in a darkened room for several days. The fear was that blindness might be the outcome of the illness and the darkened room technique was standard practice in the attempt to minimise the risk.

On the first day back at school after my spell in bed, I was sent to the children's clinic to undergo the most dreaded of all medical treatment – having 'drops' put in the eyes prior to examination by the school doctor.

It was always a nasty experience that left the recipient with hazy vision and a feeling of nausea for several hours. I never did discover why they did it or why it had to be repeated over a period of several weeks, although I suppose it had something to do with dilating the pupils of the eyes so that the medical officer could take a better look at them.

If that were not bad enough, the ordeal was made even less bearable by the fact that the person who carried out the eye drops routine was the fearsome Nurse Craven. he was a tiny woman but she possessed a powerful, dominating personality that made her young patients tremble in her presence. Her manner was curt, her tongue was sharp, and she brooked no nonsense. I had the feeling she could read our innermost thoughts.

The school's clinic was housed in a converted outbuilding in the grounds of the old manor house, near the parish church. Surrounded by neatly clipped lawns, yew trees and shrubs, the clinic had a delightful setting, but inside it was stark and bare. The walls were painted a dirty grey colour and there was an ever-present smell of disinfectant and carbolic soap.

Those of us summoned for the eye-drop treatment had to sit on a wooden bench in the cold surgery and wait to be called to a little side room, where Nurse Craven sat like a spider under a leaf near its web.

The doctor was a nice man, but by the time he came to take a look at us we were in too great a state of discomfort and misery to appreciate his gentle ministrations.

The outcome of all this was that it was decided that I needed spectacles – an awful blow to my pride. In those days no schoolboy worth his salt liked to wear glasses. It was a stigma and inevitably meant that your enemies, in moments of dispute, would sneeringly dismiss you as 'Four-eyes'.

The frustration of not being able to complete my set of Famous Cricketers, coupled with the indignity of having to face my peers in a pair of steel-rimmed specs, induced in me a feeling of depression that was difficult to shake off. Even the luxury of my favourite type of chocolate, a whipped cream walnut, which my mother bought me in an attempt to lift my spirits, did not do the trick.

There was only one thing to do in such a mood of black despair – pay a visit to Grandma Bassett. I could always count on her to raise me from the depths.

Grandma Bassett, my late father's mother, was a delicate lady with rosy cheeks and hardly a wrinkle to give an indication of her age. But her hair was pure white and she wore it in a bun, giving her the reassuring look of the archetypal grandmother.

Like her neighbours in Palmerston Street, she was preoccupied with cleanliness – at least as far as outward appearances for the benefit of the rest of the community were concerned. She seemed to be forever scrubbing the front doorstep or cleaning the windows, upstairs and down.

As with a good number of her elderly neighbours in this narrow back street of terraced houses, she had a special uniform for these domestic chores. It consisted of an apron made of rough sacking, which was tied on with string, and a flat cap, which she kept firmly in place in windy weather with a traditional hat pin.

One of my great joys was to walk along Palmerston Street and watch these ladies cleaning their upstairs windows. They all seemed to do this job at the same time. The reason was simple: if one began the operation the others felt duty-bound to follow suit.

They had a special way of dealing with the outside of the first-floor windows. They would raise the lower window, ease themselves out backwards, with their buckets and cloths, so that they could sit on the sill, and then pull down the frame tight against their thighs to make sure they did not fall to the pavement below.

There they would sit, caps on heads, polishing industriously and calling across to each other to pass on the latest titbits of gossip. Their conversations, which floated loud and clear across the cobbled street, were seldom cheerful. They were mainly concerned with death and illness. There was never any need to read the obituary column of the local newspaper.

News of tragic events in the lives of neighbouring families, and even those farther afield, passed swiftly by word of mouth, accompanied by much shaking of heads and knowing reactions like, 'Well, it was a blessed release' or 'I could see it coming months ago.'

Strangely enough, despite these high level chats, and the

occasional conversations in the corner shop, the old ladies of Palmerston Street rarely mixed socially or visited each other's homes. The age of popping round to the neighbours for morning coffee was a long way off. Instead, the time-honoured principle of 'keeping yourself to yourself' was strictly observed.

Grandma Bassett wore her sacking apron most of the time. It was an all-purpose garment that, among other things, preserved the cleanliness of her mandatory black dress.

One of the few occasions when it was not in use was Friday tea-time, when it was replaced by a well-starched apron with a colourful pattern of flowers.

Friday was pay-day and Grandma always wore her pristine apron for this all-important event. This sartorial extravagance was intended to complement the special tea she would prepare for her husband and two grown-up sons on the eagerly awaited day.

During the rest of the working week, tea consisted of slices of bread and jam and a piece of home-made plain cake, which used to be baked at the beginning of the week and therefore became somewhat stale by the end of it.

But Fridays were something out of the ordinary. There would be thinly-cut pieces of ham on every plate, and in the centre of the table, taking pride of place, would be a pile of shop-bought cakes shaped like the diamonds in a pack of cards. They were pink and yellow in colour with creamy icing on the top.

I always ran to Grandma Bassett's house after school on Fridays because she let me have one of the cakes and I would sit in a corner and eat it as I watched my grandfather and two uncles arrive home from work.

They would come in more or less at the same time, cast approving glances at the spread on the table, and then open their pay packets and lay before Grandma their financial contributions towards the family's housekeeping costs.

It was a ritual they all enjoyed and there was an air of jollity around the table as they ate their meal – at least as jolly as this rather morose family ever became.

I was a regular visitor to Grandma Bassett's house but my mother never entered it from the day of my father's funeral.

We used to live there when my father was alive. In fact he used the small front room as his barber's shop. My mother and Grandma Bassett never did see eye to eye, and with my father's death we moved out to begin our nomadic existence.

I learned many years later that, although we were not banished from the house in Palmerston Street, we were not encouraged to stay. My mother took the hint and much offence, and so we left.

On my frequent visits Grandma asked me questions that I thought were odd at the time. She would say, 'Do you have a proper breakfast before you go to school?' or 'Is that the only shirt you've got?' I did not understand why she wanted to know. Equally, I did not understand why she never mentioned my mother's name.

My mother, on the other hand, always wanted to know what Grandma and the others had had to say to me. She never prevented me going to the house in Palmerston Street but I felt that she did not like it very much. Somehow it seemed as though I let her down by going there so often.

It was a long, long time before I became fully aware of the gulf between the Bassetts and my mother, and it saddened me. Looking back, it is difficult to see why there should have been such animosity between them. After all, my mother was a kind-hearted woman who only donned a hard-natured armour to protect us both during the hard years, and my grandmother was, without doubt, the most generous person I have met in the whole of my life.

Her generosity was so pronounced that I am convinced she would willingly have given away anything she owned if she had been asked. She would regularly slip a halfpenny or a penny into my hand when I was leaving – making sure that no other member of the household saw her do it. From that it can be gathered that she was also secretive, a characteristic that never deserted her throughout her days.

On one occasion I met up with a school pal named Bernard, who lived near my Aunt Elsie. Bernard was one of the fortunate few who were never short of a penny or two and on this day he looked particularly affluent as he walked towards me, flipping a sixpence into the air and catching it with a flourish.

'I'm off to buy a tortoise,' he said.

Envy welled up within me, but I tried not to show it.

'Where are you getting it from?' I asked.

'The Gordon Road Pet Shop,' he said. 'Want to come with me?'

'How much are they?' I asked.

Bernard waved the silver tanner under my nose.

'Sixpence,' he said. 'My gran gave me the money.'

I had always wanted to own a tortoise but a tanner was so far out of my price range that I had never dared to think about buying one.

Although it was not on the direct route to the pet store, I told Bernard that I had to call to see Grandma Bassett on the way.

By the time we reached the house I had formulated a plan. Grandma looked pleased to see me but was surprised that I was accompanied by Bernard. I seldom took friends to Palmerston Street. I liked to keep its comforts and treats just for me alone.

'Have you got a paper bag I can have, Grandma?' I said.

'Whatever for?'

'Bernard's gran has given him sixpence to buy a tortoise and we want a paper bag to take it home in,' I replied with all the subtlety of a sledgehammer.

A little smile flickered across Grandma's face. She picked up her purse from the mantelpiece and took out a shining sixpenny piece.

'Would you like one as well?' she said.

I took the coin gratefully but shamelessly. More than likely it constituted the only money in her purse, but she gave it to me without hesitation.

For all her saintly ways, though, Grandma Bassett had a secret vice, although it was hardly a sin by even the harshest standards and it was certainly no secret as far as the family members were concerned.

The truth of the matter was that Grandma liked a drink, especially beer, and she imbibed a pint or two most nights, financing the habit by juggling with the housekeeping money. She kept the ale, fetched from a nearby off-licence, in a large jug in the pokey pantry at the rear of the kitchen.

The pantry was dark and had a musty odour and she would stand there taking hefty draughts, blithely believing that the rest of the family did not know what she was up to.

But they did know – and had known for years. She gave the game away so easily that even I knew what was going on. Five or six times during the course of an evening she would put down her knitting or sewing, make an excuse about checking something in the kitchen, and head for the pantry for her liquid refreshment. On her return to the living room she would wipe her mouth with a little lace handkerchief dappled with cologne, believing, I am sure, that it would help to reduce the smell of alcohol on her breath.

To their eternal credit, her husband and two sons, my Uncle Dick and Uncle Sid, never embarrassed her by even hinting that they were aware of her unorthodox drinking habits. Perhaps they were too embarrassed to mention it.

On the night of my great depression I had stayed longer at my grandmother's house than I had planned, and I set off for home (currently Aunt Kate's spare room) at a steady jogtrot.

It was turned nine o'clock and quite dark. At the bottom of Palmerston Street, where Mr Cox's grocery shop stood, was a lamppost, and jostling about in its light was a crowd of youngsters. As I drew nearer I could hear them shouting words of encouragement and then I saw two boys engaged in a fist fight.

The bout was only mildly physical, both lads being more concerned with not being hit than by actually delivering blows on their own account.

I stood on the fringe of the crowd and watched. A tall, thin boy with a long, pointed nose stepped forward and rang a bicycle bell. It was Lennie Cunliffe, who was in the same class as me at school.

'End of round two,' he announced. It was then I realised that this was no off-the-cuff street scrap. It was a well-planned affair.

Lennie Cunliffe, you see, was a born organiser. He was always arranging things – marbles contests, kite-flying marathons, inter-street football matches, or amateur talent competitions in his dad's big allotment shed.

When it came to sporting or theatrical ventures, Lennie was at the centre of things. He was an entrepreneur in the making, an embryo Florenz Ziegfeld or Tex Rickard. Like all good impresarios, he always made sure he was in pocket at the end of every venture. And his currency, like everybody else's, was the cigarette card.

While the two pugilists were having a welcome between-rounds breather, Lennie took a wad of cigarette cards from his pocket and started to count them.

It was at this point that a rather fat boy wearing a Balaclava helmet walked over to me and shouted in my ear: 'Push off, Four-eyes!'

'It's a free country,' I replied. 'I've as much right to stay here as you have.'

The fat boy, whose name was Barry Elmore, was ready with his answer to that one.

'No you have not, Four-eyes,' he yelled. 'You can only watch this fight if you pay ten fag cards entrance fee – like we all have.'

Lennie stopped counting his cards and came across to us.

'Barry's right,' he said. 'Give us ten cards and you can stay to watch.'

'I haven't got any photes with me,' I said.

'In that case, push off, Four-eyes,' cried the fat boy, giving me a shove in the ribs. Immediately I pushed him in return and we stood glaring at each other, looking quite ferocious, I dare say, in the distorting light and shadows created by the street lamp.

'Hang on a minute,' said Lennie, his talent for organising coming to the fore. 'Tell you what, why don't you two have a fight? Fifty fag cards for the winner.'

He swung round and addressed the crowd. 'We've got a grudge fight here,' he shouted. 'Ten photes each to watch a genuine grudge match!'

The majority of the boys fell over themselves to give Lennie the ticket price he had named. They were like putty in his hands when it came to audience manipulation.

While Lennie was whipping up the enthusiasm, I was making the decision to tell him that I did not want to take part in this fight. It would be a humiliating climb-down, but there were times when pacifism made good sense – and this was one of those times.

I was about to make my verbal submission when I noticed the top car in the pile in Lennie's hand. Wonder of wonders, it was the one depicting the elusive Bill Woodfull.

'Is that the prize money?' I asked.

'Yes,' said Lennie. 'And there will be a bonus of ten photes for a knockdown.'

The lure of the Bill Woodfull card was too much. I aban-

29

doned my 'peace at any price' policy and agreed to the contest. Barry Elmore did not need any encouragement. He had been ready for action from the start.

Having decided to abandon the fight that had been in progress when I arrived, Lennie beckoned the fans around him.

'Form a circle,' he ordered, and proceeded to outline the rules of the contest. 'Three rounds, three minutes each round,' he declared. He did not possess a watch, so I assumed that the duration of each round would be left to his discretion.

'Don't forget to take your specs off,' said Lennie, who never failed to show a fine regard for the welfare of his performers.

I removed my glasses and put them on the window sill of Mr Cox's shop. Barry was beginning to look bigger and stronger by the second and only the thought of Bill Woodfull stiffened my resolve to see this pugilistic encounter through to the bitter end, whatever the outcome.

My opponent and I stood eyeing each other in the centre of the circle, fists clenched and raised and heads swaying from side to side – just as we had seen Max Baer do it in the cinema newsreels.

The crowd began to tire of the inaction. They wanted value for their ten cigarette cards.

'Get on with it!' one of them shouted.

I decided not to prolong the agony any longer. If there was pain to come, I might as well get it over and done with. Throwing caution to the winds, I dashed at the fat boy, fists flailing like a windmill. The assault took him by surprise and he backed off to the wall of the shop, covering his head with his arms to ward off the blows.

For a few fleeting seconds I thought I had the measure of him, but Barry was made of sterner stuff. He withstood my initial attack and them retaliated with gusto, his knuckles peppering my unprotected face.

The inevitable happened and blood began to pour from my

nose. The crowd hooted their appreciation. There was nothing they liked better than a good nosebleed.

Just when it seemed that a monumental thrashing was to be my lot, a large figure emerged from the darkness and pushed through the crowd. It was Barry's father.

Mr Elmore was a big, lumbering man who had never been seen to laugh in public and who had few friends, but it was generally conceded in the neighbourhood that he had no peers when it came to growing vegetables.

'Pack it in!' he shouted.

He grabbed me by the shoulder and hurled me against the shop window. 'Leave our Barry alone, you little bully,' he roared, completely overlooking the fact that our Barry was doing very nicely and had not got a mark on him.

Most of the spectators scattered, including Lennie, taking with him the gate receipts and the prize money.

'If I catch you hitting our Barry again, I'll give you a clip round the ear,' threatened Mr Elmore, before putting a protective arm round the shoulders of his smirking son and leading him away from the battlefield.

As for me, I set off for Aunt Kate's house, vainly trying to stem the blood as it dripped off my chin on to my jacket. I pondered on the retribution that awaited me when I reached my temporary home.

I knew that my mother would be angry because I was late. She would also be upset by the sight of my bleeding nose, which, in turn, would make her even more angry with me for getting myself in such a mess.

So it turned out. She was standing on the doorstep when I reached Aunt Kate's modest but neatly maintained house next door to the boot and shoe factory in Nelson Street.

I was hustled up the narrow stairs leading to the back bedroom that constituted our home and my explanation of events was received without much sympathy. The judgement was that I had brought it on myself, and, as expected, I received a couple of smart slaps on the backs of my legs for my pains. But worse was to come.

'Where are your glasses?' asked my mother.

I had forgotten all about them. The excitement of the fight, the shock of Mr Elmore's interjection, and worry about my mother's reaction to the whole sorry business had driven from my mind all thoughts of that pair of spectacles. I had left them on the window sill of Mr Cox's shop.

My mother's anger boiled up again and she cuffed both my ears. I was beginning to feel that I had taken enough physical punishment for one night and I made a hasty attempt to explain where the glasses were.

'They'll be gone by now,' said my mother, ever the pessimist, adding in direct contradiction, 'You go back there and get them before somebody pinches them.'

As I ran back to Mr Cox's shop, snow began to fall, settling immediately. There was already a thin layer on the window sill by the time I arrived, but there was no sign of my spectacles. Looking around, I saw them on the pavement, glinting in the light of the street lamp. I must have knocked them off the sill when Mr Elmore pushed me against the window. Picking them up and wiping off the flakes of snow, I was horrified to see that one of the lenses was cracked. Somebody must have trodden on it in the mass exodus that followed Mr Elmore's dramatic appearance.

My first thought was that I was in line for more trouble at home. What could I say in my defence this time? Then I remembered once hearing Uncle Jack say that nobody in this country could be tried and punished twice for the same crime.

That being so, I thought, as I had been punished once for losing my glasses, there was a fair chance that I would not receive another dose of the same medicine if I returned home and said that I could not find them. And with a bit of luck I might not be fitted up with another pair.

Hoping for the best, and with nothing to lose, I dropped the spectacles down the nearest street drain and headed back to Aunt Kate's.

Happily for me, my reasoning proved sound. My mother accepted the loss with a shake of her head and neither said nor did any more about it.

When I returned to school, no one in authority made any comment on the fact that I was no longer bespectacled, and, even more surprising, I was never recalled to the school's clinic for more eye tests.

Somehow, I had slipped through the education system's bureaucratic net and my days of wearing glasses were over – at least until advancing years took their toll and I was glad of their artificial aid.

The day after the big fight outside Mr Cox's shop, I went in search of Lennie Cunliffe. There was the little matter of the prize money, including the much-desired card picturing Bill Woodfull.

Lennie was in his dad's shed and did not look very pleased with life. I said I had come to collect the purse.

'You're not entitled to it,' said Lennie, shaking his head. 'You were losing, and it was a winner-takes-all scrap.'

'I might have been losing,' I replied, 'but it was Mr Elmore who stopped the fight. It was a bit like a second throwing in the towel. If a second throws in the towel in a proper fight, then the other boxer is the winner. That's only fair.'

Lennie saw the logic of my argument but made no attempt to give me the 50 cigarette cards.

'Come on,' I said, trying to sound aggressive. 'Hand them over. They're mine by rights.'

'Can't do it,' said Lennie. 'I've lost 'em. In fact. I've lost all of 'em. I haven't got a fag card to my name.'

He then proceeded to tell me the sad story. It appeared that only that morning he had met Ralph Francis, a boy from Park View School on the other side of town.

Like Lennie, he was one of nature's organisers, a would-be impresario with a taste for gambling. The latter was understandable as Ralph's father was Whitey Francis, a bookie's runner, who conducted his furtive business while wearing a camel-hair coat and a pork-pie hat. Whitey was a spiv before the word spiv was invented, and Ralph was a chip off the old block.

Lennie also liked a bet, so when Ralph suggested a wager involving cigarette cards, he fell for it at once.

Ralph asked Lennie how many cigarette cards he had in his possession. Lennie foraged through his pockets and came up with 210 – a formidable stake by any standards.

Having counted out a similar number of cards from a biscuit tin that served as his bank vault, Ralph pointed to an alleyway on the other side of the street and said, 'Bet you can't guess what sort of animal will run out of that entry next – a dog or a cat.'

Lennie told me that he was taken aback by the bizarre nature of the wager but felt that his reputation would be in danger if he backed down.

He thought about it for a few seconds, desperately trying to remember how many dogs in relation to cats he had seen in this part of town. He concluded that he had no idea and simply made a guess.

'It'll be a dog,' he said crossing his fingers behind his back.

'In that case, I say it will be a cat,' said Ralph.

They waited patiently for a four-legged creature to emerge from the alleyway. After about five minutes a black and white cat shot out of the entry and raced up the street.

'You lose,' said Ralph, putting Lennie's 210 cards in his biscuit tin.

He had the manner of a lad who had had no doubts about the

outcome of the wager – and with good cause. Some weeks later Lennie discovered he had been hoodwinked.

While Ralph and Lennie were striking the bet, Ralph's younger brother was standing at the other end of the alleyway with the family's pet dog and cat on leads.

As soon as Lennie had named his choice of animal – a dog – Ralph sent a pre-arranged hand signal to his brother, instructing him to release the cat. It was a primitive but effective sting that worked on more than one occasion for the Francis boys.

Lennie related the tale with a catch in his voice. The loss of 210 cigarette cards was a savage blow, even though, technically, 50 of them belonged to me.

I was no less upset. I had come within an ace of obtaining the Bill Woodfull card, only to have it snatched from my grasp at the last minute.

Still, as it turned out, even if the card had come into my possession, I would not have had a complete set of Famous Cricketers – far from it. When I reached home that day I went to the drawer in the old cupboard where I kept the other 49 in the series. It was then I discovered that a broody white mouse had chewed them to pieces while trying to build itself a nest.

But that's another story.

THE JAILBIRD FROM
THE CO-OP

PROBABLY THE MOST pleasant flight of fancy for working-class men and women in the Thirties was the prospect of a windfall, sudden or anticipated, financial or in kind. Only rarely did such dreams become reality, but when they did they brought unbounded joy to the recipients.

Windfalls took various forms, the classic, of course, being the huge win on the football pools. Few people could actually claim to know anyone who had pulled off the monetary coup of a lifetime, but it was generally accepted that, every week, someone, somewhere, went from pauper to prince overnight.

Much as they would have been ecstatic over winning just one of the minor prizes on the coupon, many folk thought that 'doing the pools' was a somewhat seedy way of striving for instant affluence.

The same went for betting on racehorses. To be seen hanging around a bookmaker's office too often was a sure way to earn a reputation as a layabout not to be trusted.

Buying raffle tickets was another matter altogether. There was something honourable and decent about this means of looking for a little windfall, for then, as now, the underlying objective of the organisers was to raise funds for a good cause.

Those who bought raffle tickets felt that they were doing some deserving charity a 'good turn' and winning a prize themselves was a reward from above for their basic philan-thropy.

There was another way of earning a windfall but it was a long-term process, costing a fair amount of money over the years and calling for a resolute spirit in order to stick with it to the end. It took the form of investing in an endowment policy and had a special appeal for those who believed in budgeting for the dreaded 'rainy day'.

It was while my mother and I were lodging with Uncle Walt and Aunt Nell at 23, Branwell Street that the harmless pursuit of windfalls brought me into contact with two remarkable characters. One of them, indirectly and innocently, landed me in trouble with the law; the other, directly and forcefully, helped to clear my reputation.

Their names were Arthur Palmer and Fred Tailby, and the contrasts in their personalities and working practices could not be more marked.

Mr Palmer was an insurance agent who would never try to put pressure on a would-be client. It was against his easy-going, understanding nature to bulldoze people into taking on more financial commitments than he felt they could afford.

Mr Tailby was a travelling librarian and he took the opposite view, milking his customers for all he could get. He toured the town and nearby villages in a black and red car which was full of suitcases containing novels.

When he reached the home of a customer he would drag a couple of cases from the back seat, march in after a per-functory rap on the front door, throw open the cases to reveal the volumes and announce, 'There's some good reading in here.'

It cost twopence a week to hire a book and Mr Tailby made it his business to talk his more vulnerable clients into taking out three or four at a time. The result was that some of the slower readers had to sit up half the night to complete the stories before

Mr Tailby's next visit. The old saying, 'Waste not, want not,' applied to everything in life in those days.

Romances, family dramas, detective tales and Western adventures formed the bulk of Mr Tailby's literary offerings, with authors like Ethel M. Dell, Warwick Deeping, Edgar Wallace and Zane Grey in great demand.

We had been staying with Aunt Nell for only a few days when I had my first encounter with Mr Palmer. It was a Friday night, traditional time for collecting the weekly premiums on a family's modest policies. The insurance companies were well aware that pay day was the ideal time to make the collections. By the middle of the following week the money set aside may have had to be used for more immediate purposes and the dire spiral of arrears and possible cancellation of policies might begin.

Most households managed to avoid the trap, but only out of fear that a lapsed policy meant no pay-out to cover funeral expenses – the final humiliation. Some far-thinking people took out endowment policies within days of their offspring being born. These would mature when the child reached 16, 18 or 21. The outlay was only twopence or threepence per week but the thought of a lump sum of 50 or 60 quid in a few years' time made it an attractive proposition. When such policies reached fruition, all members of the family benefited in one way or another. There might be a new suit for father, a nice dress for mother, a trip to the seaside for everybody. It was a long wait for such a bounty, but when the day came it was one of celebration.

The town where I grew up seemed to be crowded with insurance agents. Most of them cycled from client to client. They turned out in all weathers, with their money satchels strung over their shoulders and their entry books safely tucked away in their saddle bags. Competition was keen and consequently most of them developed a persuasive line in salesmanship as they battled to beat the opposition. They would think nothing of spending a whole evening trying to talk the head of a family into taking out a shilling a month policy. It was hard work, but an honourable career that earned them respect in the community. Everybody knew they were needed in the scheme of things.

Odd man out in this enterprising breed was Arthur Palmer, a musician by training and a gentleman by nature. He did not belong to the 'hard sell' school. In fact, he did not belong to any school at all. He was unique.

Wearing a brown trilby hat with a broad brim and a round crown, a grey mackintosh and pin-striped trousers, he was a familiar figure as he cycled on his collection round. Unlike his rivals in the insurance business, he never appeared to be in a hurry. He smiled a lot and raised his hat to practically every woman he passed. This preoccupation with the simple courtesies meant that he sometimes fell off the machine, but this did not deter him.

I was in a contented mood that Friday night when I had my initial introduction to the gentle, unorthodox ways of Mr Palmer. I was sitting on a mat in front of the fire, reading a comic, and my mother was upstairs in our room, looking for a pair of gloves she had mislaid. Aunt Nell sat at the dining table, which, when not in use for meals, was covered by a green velvet cloth with gold tassels all round the edges.

Set out on the table were three insurance paying-in books and in front of each stood a small pile of coins. The total amount involved could not have been more than one shilling and ninepence but it represented a reasonably secure future. While those policies remained valid, the Swinglers were safe from future penury.

Having finished my comic, I sat looking at Aunt Nell. She had black hair, dark eyes and an olive-coloured skin that gave her a Spanish look. She must have been a bright and vivacious

40

woman when younger, but years hunched over a stitching machine in a boot factory had dulled her, mentally and physically.

By current standards, she and Uncle Walt were not too badly off, both of them having had jobs all their working lives. The fact that they had not had any children to feed and clothe had added to their relative prosperity. This modest affluence was reflected by Aunt Nell's clothes. She always dressed well, passing on garments to my mother when they fell out of fashion. My mother did not mind wearing her cast-offs because, as she used to say, 'Our Nell knows good quality when she sees it.'

There was one sartorial item that would never be passed down – Aunt Nell's fur coat. I never knew whether it was made of real fur or imitation, but it looked magnificent, and some of the women who lived in Branwell Street were green with envy. Aunt Nell was well aware of this and she wore the coat on every possible occasion – even in the summer, when it must have roasted her.

I was thinking about the fur coat when there was a gentle tap on the front door. Aunt Nell hurried down the corridor to let in Mr Palmer. He came into the living room, holding his trilby against his chest. It was his gesture of respect on entering a client's house. He sat on the piano stool and placed his hat on the floor between his feet. I expected him to produce his master payment book, scoop up the money, and set off on his travels. Not a bit of it:

'Would you like a cup of tea, Mr Palmer?' said Aunt Nell.

'I'd love one, Mrs Swingler, if it's not too much trouble,' he replied.

'It's never too much trouble for you, Mr Palmer.'

'That's nice of you, Mrs Swingler.'

The pleasantries continued throughout the tea-drinking session and still Mr Palmer made no move to complete the transaction that had brought him to number 23.

41

The conversation ranged over a variety of subjects – the weather, Benito Mussolini, births, marriages, deaths. I did not know what they were talking about half the time, but, with the inbuilt curiosity of all children, I listened intently while pretending to re-read my comic.

After about half an hour, Uncle Walt came into the room. He had been in his shed at the bottom of the garden, where he had been tacking new soles onto a pair of old shoes. He was genuinely pleased to see the visitor.

'Come on, Mr Palmer,' he said, nodding towards the piano. 'How about giving us a tune?'

Mr Palmer looked at the pendulum clock on the far wall and compared its time with his own chain watch, which he plucked from an inside breast pocket.

'Well, just one then,' he said. 'What shall it be?'

'The Poet and Peasant Overture,' said Uncle Walt, without hesitation.

Three quarters of an hour later, Mr Palmer was still at the keyboard. He had played a selection of hit songs from the Great War, including a double helping of 'Keep the Home Fires Burning', with Uncle Walt singing the words, and a couple of pieces I had never heard before but which he described as 'light classics'.

My mother had come downstairs as soon as she heard the music and, like me, sat entranced by it all. It was as if a show was being put on just for us.

Eventually, Mr Palmer turned away from the keys.

'How about you giving us a tune, Mrs Swingler?' he said coaxingly.

'Oh, I don't know,' said Aunt Nell, displaying a coyness that seemed out of character.

'Yes, play us "I'll See You Again",' said Uncle Walt, obviously enjoying himself.

With mock reluctance, Aunt Nell took over from Mr Palmer

on the piano stool and the tunes began to flow again. It was well past nine o'clock when she finally shut down the piano lid.

'Have a bit of bread and cheese before you go, Mr Palmer?' she asked.

'Only a little, Mrs Swingler,' he replied.

Out came a cheese dish, half a dozen thick slices of crusty bread and a round glass bowl containing what was always referred to as 'best' butter.

We all joined in the simple but delicious supper. Uncle Walt said it was better than a five-course meal at the top hotel in the town. Nobody disagreed with him.

At long last, Mr Palmer counted the coins and placed them in the satchel that had hung round his neck for the whole evening. With a flourish of his fountain pen he filled in the paying-in books and handed them to Aunt Nell.

'Thank you, Mrs Swingler.'

'Thank you, Mr Palmer.'

With that, Mr Palmer left the house and mounted his bicycle, which he had left propped against the front room window. He had been at number 23 for more than three hours.

As the weeks rolled by, I was to learn that the piano playing sessions were regular events at the Swingler household, although they did not always last as long as the first one I was privileged to witness.

I could not help wondering how on earth Mr Palmer ever completed his rounds if he made a habit of dallying at other homes on his books.

It's a fair bet that promotion never came his way, but, being a man completely without ambition, he probably never wanted it. Nevertheless, he was a marvellous ambassador for the insurance business.

While Mr Palmer confined himself to music, polite conversation and, when pushed, the financial transactions of his employers, Mr Fred Tailby was involved in many extra activities to supplement what must have been a meagre income from book lending.

The boot of his car was usually packed with such items as bars of soap, boxes of chocolates, pairs of silk stockings and tins of corned beef, which he sold at considerably less than shop price. There was no doubting that they were bargains and most customers were happy to accept his assurances that everything was above board.

Mr Tailby was also an enthusiastic seller of raffle tickets, and the very nature of his job made him an ideal purveyor of these possible passports to brief prosperity.

The first time I saw him he was trying to sell tickets to Uncle Walt on behalf of the British Legion. It was the Christmas fur and feather raffle and the prize list he read out sounded very tempting – rabbits, hares, pheasants, cockerels, ducks, geese.

Uncle Walt could not resist the chance. The tickets were threepence each and he produced a shilling in order to buy four.

'You never know your luck, Walt,' said Mr Tailby. 'What could be better than a nice bird for Christmas?'

He was busy stacking books into his suitcases when my mother came in from the kitchen.

'How about you, my duck?' he said with the easy familiarity that was his stock in trade. 'Would you like to buy some raffle tickets? It's for a good cause.'

She poked about in her purse as he assured her the tickets were good value at threepence each, bearing in mind the quality and range of the prizes.

'I'll have one,' she said, bringing out two pennies and two halfpennies.

'Why not?' said Mr Tailby. 'You've got just as good a chance

44

with one ticket as 50. After all, they only draw out one ticket at a time.'

Uncle Walt said he could not understand the reasoning behind that observation, but looked as though he wished he had not bothered to buy four.

Having pocketed the money, Mr Tailby carefully wrote the names and address on the counterfoils. 'I'll let you know if you have won anything,' he said, sitting down on the piano stool and looking through the open door into the kitchen, where Aunt Nell was brewing a cup of tea. Unlike Mr Palmer, Mr Tailby was not usually invited to join the Swinglers in a cup of their favourite beverage, but he was skilled in the art of dropping heavy hints and there were times when they made the offer, which, of course, he never refused. This was one of them.

Apparently, neither Aunt Nell nor Uncle Walt liked him very much, the former because he had a cheeky line in conversation with the ladies, particularly the married ones. Even what appeared to be innocent remarks had Max Millerish undertones.

Uncle Walt's mild distaste for him was connected with his habit of telling tall tales about his exploits in the trenches during the Great War. Mark you, the night he sold my mother the raffle ticket he looked every inch the ex-soldier of distinction. He was tall and well-built, with broad shoulders that were enhanced by the padding in his overcoat. He also had an officer-type moustache, though Uncle Walt told me later that he had never risen above the rank of lance-corporal.

The fact that he was selling raffle tickets for the British Legion gave him the opportunity to recall more memories of his days on the Western Front.

It did not worry me that his stories might be fabrications. It was enough that they were exciting and gory. I sat in my chair in the corner and listened intently to his description of the incident in which his platoon opened fire with small arms against Baron

45

von Richthofen, who was flying low near their position in the line. Mr Tailby claimed that the German air ace crashed soon after this action.

'It makes you think,' said Mr Tailby, speaking from behind a haze of Woodbine smoke. 'It might have been my bullet that shot down the Red Baron. Yes, it makes you think.'

Judging by the sceptical look on Uncle Walt's normally expressionless face, it certainly made him think. His manner confirmed that he did not have much faith in the validity of the book lender's war stories. Some time later I heard Uncle Walt tell Aunt Nell, 'People who did things out there never talk about them.'

Exactly a week after this visit Mr Tailby turned up again on the doorstep of number 23. He had a suitcase in each hand and a white envelope was sticking out of his overcoat pocket.

He looked elated, like a bearer of glad tidings. As it happened, it was my mother who opened the front door to him, so he was able to deliver his good news without delay.

'You're a winner, Mrs Bassett,' he announced, pushing past her and heading for the front room where Uncle Walt and Aunt Nell were sitting listening to their wireless.

'What's up?' asked Uncle Walt, plainly annoyed at being disturbed.

'Mrs Bassett has won a prize in the Legion raffle,' said Mr Tailby. 'What do you reckon to that then?'

The wireless was switched off and we all looked at the visitor, awaiting more information on the surprise windfall.

'What's she won?' asked Uncle Walt.

'Don't know,' said Mr Tailby. 'But there's a letter here from the secretary telling her she's won something.'

He handed the envelope to my mother and I could see that she was trembling slightly in anticipation. I could not remember her ever winning anything, so it must have been a moment of great joy for her.

She ripped open the envelope and took out a letter. It looked very important and official. We watched her read it carefully.

'Well,' said Aunt Nell, 'what have you won?'

'It doesn't say,' answered my mother. 'It just says I have won a prize in the raffle and that I can pick it up from the Co-op butchers in Regent Street.'

'I hope it's not just a rabbit,' said Uncle Walt. 'A rabbit for Christmas is not much cop.' He had already assumed that the prize, whatever it was, would be shared.

'It might be a cockerel,' said Aunt Nell cheerfully. 'They have lovely cockerels at the Co-op.'

'Never mind, sweetie,' said Mr Tailby, taking advantage of this happy occasion to put his arm round my mother's waist. 'It's a prize – that's all that matters. It's better than nothing, eh?'

They all agreed that that was the case. Delight over the fact that a windfall, however small it might be, had dropped into the Swingler household led Aunt Nell to offer Mr Tailby a cup of tea. Naturally, he accepted.

The following day, before I set off for the last day of the school term, my mother took the winning ticket from her handbag and handed it to me.

'Now,' she said, 'when you come out of school I want you to go to the Co-op and get our prize. Whatever you do, don't lose the ticket.'

The responsibility weighed heavily on me all day. I found it difficult to concentrate on what the teachers had to say and every few minutes I would feel in the back pocket of my trousers to make sure the ticket was still there. Losing that little piece of blue paper did not bear thinking about.

One of the teachers, Miss Dickerson, saw me put my hand behind my back to check on the presence of the ticket.

'That's the third time I've seen you feeling your behind,' she said. 'What's the matter? Have you got a boil coming?'

47

Miss Dickerson always assumed we had boils coming when we started to fidget in class. More often than not she was right.

'No, miss,' I said. 'Just an itch.'

'Well, don't scratch it then, or you will make it sore,' said Miss Dickerson.

My lack of concentration got me into trouble on more than one occasion during that long day and I was kept behind for half an hour as a punishment – even though it was the eve of the Christmas break.

As soon as I was released, I set off for Regent Street on the other side of the town. All the corner shops along the way were brightly illuminated and decorated to mark the festive season. Hanging from the ceilings were paper Chinese lanterns containing lighted candles, and the smell of melting wax combined with the sickly odour of paraffin heaters wafted out into the street every time a shop door opened. In those days, fire hazards did not figure highly in the thoughts of shopkeepers or shoppers.

I would have liked to stop and stare into these well-stocked windows – one of life's real treats at this magical time of the year – but I had an important mission to carry out and I could not indulge in my Christmas fantasies.

The Co-op butcher's shop was empty of customers when I arrived and the staff, uniformly clad in blue and white striped aprons, were relaxing, leaning their elbows on the rough wooden counters. Sawdust covered the floor and there were large brown patches where it had soaked up blood that had dripped from hanging meat.

I stood in the centre of the shop, clutching the little blue ticket. A man with big hands and massive forearms came out of a back room. He must have been the head butcher.

'What do you want, son?' he asked, not unkindly.

'I've come to fetch my mam's prize in the raffle,' I said.

He held out his hand. 'Give us the ticket.'

After looking at the number, he checked it against a list that was pinned to the wall. It was then he began to chuckle.

'You planning to take it home on your own?' he asked, winking at the other butchers.

'Course I am,' I replied, wondering why the head butcher thought the prospect so funny.

I soon discovered the answer to that one. The man went into the back room and returned carrying the biggest unplucked goose I had seen in my life.

Gripping the bird by the neck, the butcher held it alongside me. The staff of the Co-op, including the girl at the pay desk, roared with laughter. The goose was bigger than me.

'You'll never manage it, son,' said the head butcher. 'Better let your mam fetch it.'

'Yes, I will manage it,' I said, with all the confidence I could muster. My mother had told me to bring home the prize and I intended to do just that, even though, in my mind's eye, it was beginning to take on the proportions of an ostrich.

The butchers were still laughing when I staggered out of the shop under the weight of the monstrous bird. I held it close to me, with my arms round its back, as though we were taking part in some ludicrous dance. Its neck hung over my left shoulder and its feet kept bumping against my ankles. To make matters worse, the feathers began to irritate my nasal passages and I started to sneeze.

It was not long before I realised that this method was not going to work. So I tried to carry it over my shoulder like a sack. That was even less successful. The bird's legs and my legs became entangled every few steps.

Worn out, I sat down in a doorway to consider my next move. The goose, slumped beside me, seemed even bigger than when I first saw it in the shop.

Just when it seemed that I was beaten, I was struck by a brainwave. I remembered that Les Bonham lived only a few

49

doors from where I was sitting – and Les was the proud possessor of a bicycle. If Les would lend me his machine – and I was sure he would – I could prop the goose on the saddle and wheel it home. It was all so simple, or so I thought.

Unfortunately, Les Bonham's house was in darkness when I arrived. Ever hopeful, I knocked on the door several times, but there was no reply.

Eventually, I walked round to the back of the house and there, standing against an old mangle, was Les's bicycle. I knew immediately what I intended to do – and there was no guilt attached. I had no doubt that had Les been there he would have let me borrow the bike with a good heart. What's more, I would return the machine as soon as I had delivered the bird into my mother's safe keeping.

With conscience clear, resolve stiffened and spirits higher, I perched the goose's rear end on the saddle and hung its neck over the handlebars.

It was not as easy a task as I had thought it would be, but at least it was better than my previous mode of operation. The saddle of the bicycle was not too secure and it wobbled on occasions, causing the bird to slip off, but, taking everything into consideration, I made good progress.

As I trudged past the police station near the corner of Lenford Street and Bellington Road, still struggling to keep the goose's rear end on the loose saddle, I saw a figure standing in the lighted doorway.

It was Police Sergeant Beckett, who regularly visited our school to give road safety lessons and, I suspect, to remind would-be unruly elements that the long arm of the law stretched a considerable distance.

'Hey!' he called. 'What have you got there?'

My next action, which was foolish in the extreme, was based on the well-known fact that policemen did not speak to small boys unless they felt they were up to no good. Sergeant Beckett's question, delivered with just the right tone of powerful authority, threw me into a panic. I tried to run away, pushing the bicycle as hard as I could.

It was an ill-considered move, badly executed. The sudden burst of speed made the saddle move sideways, dislodging the goose. I took hold of the bird's neck as it slithered off the handlebars, but by this time one of its feet had become caught in the spokes of the back wheel.

This development pulled up the bike with a jerk and I tumbled into the gutter with the machine and the goose on top.

I looked up and saw Sergeant Beckett looming over me. He looked down, unsmiling and unmoved by my predicament. He made no attempt to help me to my feet. Questions came first.

'Is this your goose?' he asked.

'No, it's my mam's.'

'What are you doing giving it a ride on your bike?'

I made another mistake. 'It's not my bike,' I said.

'Not your bike? Who did you steal it from then?'

'I didn't steal it. I borrowed it,' I said. Even as I spoke the words, I knew I was plunging myself into even deeper trouble.

'I've heard that one before,' said Sergeant Beckett.

'It's Les Bonham's bike,' I said, desperately trying to rescue myself. 'He's a pal of mine.'

'Did he say you could borrow it?'

I hesitated before answering, but I knew I was trapped whatever I said. 'No, he didn't,' I mumbled, adding hopefully, 'But he would have done if I had asked him.'

'Ah, but you didn't ask him, did you? That's the point. Borrowing things without asking is stealing. Did you know that?'

'Yes, sir,' I said, tears welling into my eyes. Visions of a jail sentence on Dartmoor were beginning to cross my mind.

'Now, about this goose,' said Sergeant Beckett, having cleared

51

up the bicycle case to his own satisfaction. 'Where did that come from?'

I thought I was on safer ground with this one. He could not accuse me of stealing that as well.

'My mam won it,' I said with confidence.

'Won it, did she? That's another good excuse people use when they've got something that doesn't belong to them.'

'In a raffle,' I said, still trying to salvage something from a rapidly deteriorating situation. 'She won it in a raffle. It's for Christmas.'

'Of course it's for Christmas,' said the sergeant, a note of sarcasm entering his voice. 'The question is: Whose Christmas?'

There was silence for a few seconds while Sergeant Beckett took a close look at the goose. Eventually he pulled the bicycle off me and said, 'You had better come into the station. I want a few more words with you.'

He held the goose by the neck with one hand while he propped the bicycle against the police station wall with the other.

'Come on,' he commanded, and marched up the station steps.

I followed, feeling like one of those convicts walking to the electric chair that we used to see in American gangster pictures.

There was only one other policeman on duty. He sat at a desk filling in a form and appeared to take little interest in my arrival. But I could see he had a grin on his red face.

Sergeant Beckett went behind a desk after dumping the goose on top of the long counter that separated staff from visitors. He picked up a pencil.

'Let's have your name, sonny,' he said. With a sinking heart I realised that the judicial process was about to gather momentum.

Question followed question. All were answered truthfully but, even as I spoke, I knew my replies were sounding more and more unlikely.

'The Co-op butchers in Regent Street you say?' said Sergeant

52

Beckett, reaching for the station's telephone directory. He flipped through the pages, unclipped the earpiece from the two-section phone and dialled a number.

Hope rose within me. Surely the head butcher at the shop would confirm that I had indeed obtained the bird in legitimate fashion. There was a long pause before the sergeant put the earpiece back on its hook.

'They must have closed,' he said. 'It's getting late, you know.'

There was a lengthy silence while he gave the matter some thought. Then he picked up the bird. 'I think we had better put this in a safe place until all this is sorted out,' he said.

Instinctively I reached up over the top of the counter and gripped the goose's neck. I did not want to lose sight of my mother's raffle prize after all we had been through together. The sergeant pulled one way and I pulled the other. Despite his angry expression, I refused to let go.

'Look, sonny,' said the sergeant, obviously realising that he was beginning to appear ridiculous in the eyes of his station colleague, who was smiling even more broadly now. 'We'll just put the bird in one of the cells for the moment. It'll be quite safe until we get to the bottom of all this.'

I held on to the neck, unconvinced.

'I've even got my own Christmas dinner in there,' said Sergeant Beckett. 'That's a goose as well. Come and have a look.'

I followed him out of the door and along a corridor. There were two small cells at the end of it and in one of them was a fully-feathered goose, its head dangling over the side of a bunk bed.

The policeman put our goose on the bed and picked up the other one.

'There you are,' he said. 'That's my dinner. They'll both be all right in here.'

As he held up his bird I could see that, handsome though it

53

was, it was not as big as the one my mother had won. In fact, it looked almost puny by comparison.

'Right,' said the sergeant. 'Now we'll go back and get to the bottom of all this. What did you say your name was – Ronnie Bassett?'

I could not take any more of this inquisition. Blind panic seized me again and I turned and ran back along the corridor, into the station reception room and then down the steps into the street.

I was 50 yards away and in full flight before Sergeant Beckett appeared in the station doorway.

'Come back, you little sod!' he shouted. He was wasting his time. I had a good lead and I was determined to get back to Aunt Nell's house to tell my mother my tale of woe.

As I sprinted through the dark, empty streets, lights were blazing in the front rooms of the better-off households. I caught glimpses of boys and girls perched on piano stools practising their scales or reading comics in front of cheerful-looking coal fires. Such cosy scenes represented an alien world at that crisis-ridden moment. My only concern was the recovery of our Christmas dinner.

Aunt Nell, Uncle Walt, my mother and Mr Palmer were sitting round the table having a cup of tea when I burst into the room. My mother looked relieved to see me, but her first question was, 'Where's our prize?'

'It's in prison,' I gasped, fighting for breath after the long run. The four of them sat dumbfounded by the revelation.

'What do you mean – in prison?' said Uncle Walt.

'A policeman took it off me and put it in a cell,' I said, bursting into tears. I had come to the end of my tether.

The four waited patiently for me to get the tears out of my system and slowly, by gentle interrogation, they pieced together the full story.

Almost before I had finished, my mother was putting on her hat and coat, ready for the trip to the station.

'I'll soon put a stop to all this,' she said, looking into her handbag to make sure she had the letter confirming her right to the prize.

'Allow me to come with you, Mrs Bassett,' said Mr Palmer, quietly but firmly. My mother permitted herself a rare smile to show her appreciation of the offer.

We set off on the walk to the police station, with Mr Palmer pushing his bicycle. He kept assuring me that all would be well. I had my doubts.

Walking up the steps into the station, I stayed close to my mother. I felt I needed all the protection I could get when the time came to face Sergeant Beckett.

The man in question was standing behind the counter, a copy of the local paper open in front of him. He looked surprised to see me. Before he could speak, my mother began her verbal attack.

'What are you doing saying our Ronnie is a thief?' she demanded to know.

Before he could answer, she plucked the British Legion letter out of her handbag and slapped it on the counter.

'That's my bird,' she continued. 'Our Ronnie was only bringing it home from the shop. You read that letter. You'll see.'

Sergeant Beckett picked up the sheet of paper and read through its contents twice before handing it back. He was not prepared to surrender easily.

'How do I know that you are Mrs Bassett,' he said. 'You could be anybody. You could have found that letter.'

'Don't be silly,' said my mother. With that she produced her birth certificate, which, for some reason I never understood, she always carried in her handbag.

Sergeant Beckett gave the certificate a careful examination before handing it back with a deep sniff.

'You've got no proof that this belongs to you either,' he said. It was at this point that the mild-mannered Mr Palmer revealed a side to his personality that surprised and at the same time delighted me. He leaned across the counter, putting his face within an inch of Sergeant Beckett's.

'Considering that you have three stripes on your arm, you are a very foolish fellow,' he said. 'This good lady has given you concrete proof that she is who she says she is. What's more, I can vouch for her.'

His voice was no louder than usual but it had a steely ring to it. Sergeant Beckett looked shaken.

Mr Palmer continued. 'Now, either you give Mrs Bassett her goose or I shall go round to your superior's house and register a complaint about your unreasonable behaviour. I know Inspector Rankin well. He's married to my sister.'

The two men stared into each other's eyes for a few more seconds before Sergeant Beckett accepted defeat and broke contact.

'All right,' he said, still with some reluctance. 'I'll go and fetch the bird for you. But you tell that lad not to run away next time a policeman wants to talk to him.'

The sergeant went off to the cells and returned in a couple of minutes with the goose. My mother's face lit up. The prize was far better than she had expected.

I was not so thrilled. This bird was smaller and less plump than the one I had collected from the Co-op. It also had two perfectly formed feet, whereas the one I had struggled with on the long trek home had a piece of foot missing, the outcome of an entanglement with the spokes of the bicycle.

'It's a nice looking bird, Mrs Bassett,' said Sergeant Beckett, turning on the charm in a bid to make amends. 'That'll make you a lovely Christmas dinner.'

I came within an ace of announcing that it was the wrong goose – that our prize was bigger and better than this one. Discretion took over and I held my peace. I had made enough mistakes for one day.

Without a doubt, Sergeant Beckett had been overcome by greed and had made the switch with his own bird, but I could not face another confrontation. We would have to make do with this lesser offering, and if I kept quiet no one would be any the wiser. After all, we did have a bird – and that was all that mattered.

There was much joy in Aunt Nell's house when we returned in triumph with the goose, which my mother carried proudly through the streets while I walked beside her, wheeling Les Bonham's bicycle. Mr Palmer had offered to carry it for her, but she would have none of it.

Christmas Day was soon upon us and the festive feast laid out on Aunt Nell's table was a marvel to behold. The well-basted, brown-skinned goose occupied place of honour in the centre and there was more food on display than I had seen for ages.

Our plates were piled high with Brussels sprouts, potatoes and peas, the three grown-ups had glasses of stout to wash it all down, and I had a tumbler of Tizer.

We did not have crackers to pull and consequently there were no paper hats, because Aunt Nell did not go in for that sort of thing, but coloured paper chains were looped across the ceiling and draped around the gold-painted frame of the large mirror over the mantelpiece.

Before we sat down at the table, Aunt Nell had announced that there was a threepenny piece somewhere inside her home-made Christmas pudding and it would become the property of the one who received the slice that contained it.

Even more important, she said, the recipient would be guaranteed good luck for the whole of the coming year – prize without price in that uncertain age. She was looking at me and smiling when she made this announcement. I was not sure how it would be done, but I knew that I would be the winner.

The happiness I felt at that moment almost choked me with its intensity, but the best was yet to come. As he set about carving the goose, Uncle Walt paid me the supreme tribute.

'Seeing as you have been such a good and brave lad, I reckon you ought to have one of the legs,' he said, dropping it on to my already overcrowded plate. It was a blissful moment.

As I munched my mammoth helping of goose, I had the added pleasure of watching Uncle Walt cutting up and eating his food with the knife and fork he had taken off the dead German in the trenches.

I could not have asked for more, thinking then, as now, that it was the most delicious Christmas dinner of my life. Drinking my Tizer and savouring the unique taste of my goose leg, I was overwhelmed with a feeling of goodwill to all men.

I even managed to entertain the genuine hope that Sergeant Beckett was enjoying our goose as much as we were enjoying his.

A MIDNIGHT DATE WITH DOCTOR FRANKENSTEIN

MY MOTHER LIKED nothing more than a visit to the cinema. It was a passion she shared with millions of all ages during the Thirties.

Going to the pictures in those days was not just a question of the pursuit of colourful entertainment in an otherwise drab world. It was an escape from grim reality into a dream-world peopled by pretty dancing girls, murderous gangsters, brave cowboys, savage Indians and infallible detectives.

This comparatively inexpensive, readily available excursion into the celluloid land of fantasies was the true opium of the masses. Few members of the working classes could resist the appeal of what was commonly and affectionately known as 'three pennyworth of dark'.

Stars like Clark Gable, Greta Garbo, Ronald Colman and Myrna Loy were as familiar as the folk next door. Cinema-goers were well acquainted with their on-screen mannerisms and their private lives were an open book, thanks to the fan magazines that abounded in newsagents' shops.

The magazines were packed with interviews with the top actors and actresses of the day, and although readers did not know it at the time, the personal details they revealed were usually as fictitious as the plots of the films in which they appeared.

All sorts of myths grew up around the Hollywood celebrities

and became even more far-fetched with the telling. For example, it was rumoured among schoolboys that Boris Karloff, then making a big name for himself in horror films, was as frightening a figure in real life as he was on the screen.

Legend had it that he wandered the streets of Hollywood at night, striking fear and terror into the hearts of his fellow performers. No one, it was said, dare leave their home when he was on the loose.

I believed the story because I wanted to believe it. It was not until years later that I discovered that Mr Karloff was, in fact, a gentle, gracious man who liked to spend his leisure hours watching cricket.

But there was more to going to the pictures than the enjoyment of the films. There was the cinema itself. It did not matter whether it was of the old 'fleapit' variety, dating back to the early days of the silents, or one of the plush new palaces with silk drapes on the walls and thick, luxurious carpets. They were all irresistible, marvellous retreats for the world-weary in search of a temporary diversion.

The town where I was born boasted no fewer than five cinemas and most of them changed their programmes twice each week. The result was a feast of entertainment with a rich choice to suit all tastes.

Two of the five were old buildings, small and dusty with rickety seats and projection systems that were not always reliable. The other three were large edifices, exotically furnished and run with meticulous efficiency. The seats were comfortable, with padded arm-rests, and elaborate chandeliers hung from the ceilings. Ever-present was the sweet smell of perfume. This was provided by smartly-dressed usherettes who came round with spray guns in between performances and sometimes while the films were actually being shown. All in all, there was more comfort to be found in these magic places than in many of the poorer homes in the town.

Queues outside the cinemas were frequent, especially when top-flight stars were on display, or word of mouth had spread tidings of the high standard of a film.

It was on occasions such as these that the commissionaires came into their own. Every cinema had one of these majestic figures, even the unfairly named fleapits. The commissionaires were tall, upright men, patently former non-commissioned officers in the army. They were attired in neat, well-cut uniforms with an abundance of polished buttons. They wore their peak caps in the manner of guardsmen and their white gloves were spotless.

No one took liberties with men of such authority. There was no queue-jumping while they were on duty and their decision on who went in and who stayed out was final.

Standing on the steps of the cinema, they would await a signal that seats had been vacated and were now available. Then they would announce, 'Four seats at ninepence, two at sixpence.'

As the lucky half-dozen hurried to the pay-desk, the patient line of would-be patrons shuffled forward, pleased to be a few steps nearer their dream destination. It was all as orderly as a military parade-ground.

The commissionaires maintained their aloof stand at all times. Friends and relatives entering their cinemas or walking by the foyer entrances would never dare to stop and chat. They would restrict themselves to a brief 'hello' which, in response, would draw a nod of recognition or a quick salute from the man in uniform.

If the commissionaires represented law and order within the cinema and its precincts, the managers stood for power and affluence.

They always wore dinner jackets and bow ties and their shirts were never other than crisp and white. Their shoes were highly polished and their fingernails were manicured and clean. Strutting about the foyers and up and down the aisles, they had the superior manner of landed gentry inspecting their far-flung estates. Monarchs of all they surveyed, they were regarded with the utmost respect by the usherettes, cleaning ladies and projectionists. The manager of a cinema was a most important person in the Thirties.

He also had outright authority over the general public when it came to assessing the ages of those wishing to patronise his establishment.

In those days films fell into three categories: U, which could be seen by all age groups; A, which could not be attended by those under 16, unless accompanied by an adult; and H, which stood for horror and meant that under no circumstances could anyone below the age of 16 be allowed to watch them.

Consequently, in addition to refusing entry to unruly elements, vagrants or even scruffily dressed individuals, the manager had to weed out those trying to outwit the category rulings. He had the task of deciding the age of the hopeful at the pay desk, and his word was law.

That's not to say that under-age film fans always failed to gain admission. Some did manage to escape the eagle eyes of managers and their staffs by getting a stranger to obtain their tickets for them and then sneaking into the darkened auditorium when the usherettes were otherwise engaged.

Some ambitious youngsters would walk on the balls of their feet in an attempt to look taller or talk in a deep voice. I knew one boy who daubed a moustache on his lip with chimney soot in the hope that it made him look grown-up. Inevitably, such ploys ended in failure.

It was not easy to decide which gave those who succeeded in breaking the rules the most pleasure – the film they had defied authority to see or the satisfaction of knowing that they had beaten the system.

Even so, it was a risky business, for there was always the

chance that, as they watched the picture, the manager would appear at the end of the row and thunder, 'Come on, you – out!' Such exits were never less than embarrassing.

I was thrown out only once. It happened at my favourite cinema, the Electric Plaza, and I was in the company of my mother, who brought about the dismissal.

The Plaza was the second oldest cinema in the town and was unique in that it had no balcony. It also had a steeply sloping floor, which lent itself to a pastime very popular among the younger element. This took the form of trying to see if you could get an empty lemonade bottle to roll from the rear of the auditorium to the bottom rail. Providing feet did not get in the way, it worked more times than not.

Another feature of the Plaza before the days of continuous performances was the manager's odd habit of instructing his usherettes to open the exit doors a couple of minutes before the main film ended, presumably to cope with the rush of those less patriotic patrons who wished to get out before the National Anthem was played.

Unfortunately, the exit doors were at the side of the screen. When they were thrown open with a clatter near the end of matinees in the summer months, shafts of sunlight would blaze into the darkened auditorium, temporarily blinding the audience and making it impossible for them to see clearly the closing scene of the film. Strangely enough, no one ever complained.

My mother and I were staying with Aunt Flo and Uncle Bill in their house on the new Mill Farm council estate at the time of the unhappy incident involving the hard-boiled eggs and our ejection from the Electric Plaza.

The day had started off well, with my mother announcing that she intended to take me to the pictures that evening.

'You be waiting for me outside the factory at half past five and we will go straight to the pictures,' she said. 'If we get there nice and early we ought to get good seats.'

63

'What about tea?' I asked. Food was seldom far from my thoughts in those days.

'I've made us some sandwiches. I've got them here,' she said, holding open her tattered shopping bag so that I could see a small cardboard box inside. 'We can eat them while we are watching the film.'

'What are we going to see?'

'*It Happened One Night.* It's got Clark Gable and Claudette Colbert in it. They always take a good part.'

I groaned inwardly. I had heard about this film. It was what schoolboys used to call a 'lovey-dovey' picture. We had yet to reach the stage where we appreciated sophisticated comedy, preferring a Wild-West adventure any day.

Still, it was a trip to the cinema, and my favourite one at that – the Electric Plaza. Even if I did not like the film, I knew I would enjoy the atmosphere in this marvellous old building.

The day passed quickly enough and, as instructed, I positioned myself outside the doors of Buswell's boot factory well before checking-out time.

The factory, like so many more in boot- and shoe-producing towns, was situated in a back street, with terraced houses on either side. The pungent smell of leather drifted about the street at all times and the noise from the factory's machines was a constant disturbance for those living in the immediate vicinity.

There used to be an old saying in the town that you were more likely to get a bicycle tyre puncture in streets where there were factories than you were in those free of industrial associations. The reason, so it was said, was that when the dinner time hooter sounded, the workers would rush out into the street, anxious to get home as quickly as possible for their midday break. As they had only half an hour, every second counted in the sprint to the meal table. Diving out of the door, the male workers would spit out the unused tin tacks that they always carried in their mouths for convenience when hammering on soles. This meant there were plenty of sharp nails lying in the gutters, ready to deflate the tyres of the unwary.

I stood well to the side as half past five approached, because I knew from experience that the workers, men and women, would come pouring out like a cavalry charge as soon as the knocking-off hooter blared. They had no intention of staying in the factory any longer than necessary, and who could blame them? After all, if they turned up for work a minute late in the mornings they found the factory doors or gates locked and they had to wait 15 minutes for admittance. And that, of course, resulted in the loss of a quarter-of-an-hour's pay.

Two minutes before the hooter went off, a caretaker opened the big doors. Then came the rush, some of the men still taking off their aprons as they strode along the street.

My mother was in the vanguard of the exodus and we wasted no time in starting the long walk to the Electric Plaza in the centre of the town. As my mother had suggested, we had no difficulty in getting two 'nice' seats and I curled up in mine, ready to be entertained.

A travelogue was being shown when my mother opened her shopping bag and took out the cardboard box containing our tea. She handed me a shrimp paste sandwich. I loved shrimp paste and found it tasted even better in the dark.

The travelogue ended and the trailers for the next week's films were about to start when my mother handed me a slightly clammy, oval-shaped object. It was a hard-boiled egg with the shell removed.

'Don't drop it on the floor,' she whispered.

I looked round at her and saw her take a huge bite from her egg. As is the nature with some hard-boiled eggs, a somewhat unpleasant smell began to permeate the air around her.

The aroma did not seem to worry her in the slightest and she started on a second one as soon as she had swallowed the first.

Several people in the row in front looked over their shoulders and I could hear them muttering.

I had only just bitten the end off my egg when the manager marched up the aisle and stood looking down at the woman in the end seat of the row in front of us. In the reflected light from the screen, I could see her jaws moving, so she was obviously chewing something.

'Excuse me, madam,' said the manager. 'Are you eating hard-boiled eggs by any chance?'

The woman's shoulders heaved with indignation.

'Certainly not,' she said. 'I'm chewing a mint humbug.'

The man sitting next to her piped up.

'It's this woman behind me,' he said, flicking his thumb in our direction. 'She's the one who is eating eggs. And it's a right pong. It shouldn't be allowed.'

It was my mother's turn to receive the attentions of the manager, who was becoming angrier with every passing second.

'I cannot have this sort of thing in my cinema,' he said, doubtless trying to remember to abide by the proprietor's instructions that patrons should be treated with courtesy at all times.

'We are only having our tea,' said my mother defensively.

'This is not a restaurant,' replied the manager, swiftly disposing of that line of argument.

'Well,' said my mother, ever a doughty fighter when cornered, 'you sell ice cream and chocolate. That's eating, isn't it?'

'I'm afraid I must ask you to leave,' said the manager, refusing to be drawn on that one. 'If you don't go at once, I shall have to call the police. You are upsetting all my patrons.'

'We shall want our money back,' said my mother, rising to her feet. 'We have only seen a bit of the travelogue.'

'Yes, you can have your money back,' said the manager, relieved that the incident had not got too far out of hand.

As soon as the manager had appeared and the trouble started,

I had made an attempt to get rid of the evidence by stuffing all the egg into my mouth in one go. I was still struggling to chew it and swallow it without making myself sick as we made our inglorious exit from the Electric Plaza.

During the walk home my mother remained unrepentant.

'If they let you eat ice cream and smoke fags in a cinema, I can't see why they won't let you eat a hard-boiled egg,' she said.

I was beyond caring by this time, and when my mother said that we would return the following evening to see *It Happened One Night*, I took the coward's way out.

'Do you mind going on your own, mam?' I said. 'I've promised to go round and play at Norman Mason's house tomorrow night.'

Norman Mason was probably my best friend during that stage of my life. He lived with his widowed mother and grandmother in a council house in the next street.

His mother's garden and Aunt Flo's back garden butted on to each other and we struck up a cheerful friendship after getting into conversation over the wire fence dividing the two properties.

He was a true and loyal companion, strong and fearless and a genuine lover of animals. He had one fault, though. He could not keep a secret or respect a confidence.

Tell Norman something very private and personal and you could guarantee that everyone else of his acquaintance would know about it within 24 hours. It was like having a town crier for a pal. He was not a 'snitch' or a tell-tale; he just enjoyed passing on information. It would not have surprised me if he had become a newspaper reporter or a news announcer on the wireless when he grew up.

It was my friendship with Norman that sparked off a midnight adventure involving one of my much-loved town cinemas and provided me with another insight into the bizarre world of grown-ups.

It all started while I was having tea with Aunt Flo and Uncle Bill. The latter was reading the local evening newspaper as he munched thick slices of bread and strawberry jam.

His eyesight was not all that good, either at close range or for distances, and consequently his head was bent low over the paper as he read.

He had a habit of reading out stories for the benefit of Aunt Flo, who liked to know the local gossip but could not be bothered to read it for herself. Uncle Bill would read out the headlines and then the stories, punctuating many items with his own comments, which were liberally laced with swear words.

He had peculiar views on most subjects, usually finishing each observation with expressions like 'Bloody cheek!' or 'Sod that for a game of soldiers!'

He was in full spate that particular tea-time and, as usual, I was enjoying every minute of it.

'Hell's bells, Flo, listen to this!' he said, and proceeded to read out a story about the Regal Cinema, which was due to show a horror-film double bill the following week – *Frankenstein* and *Dracula*.

The story revealed that the manager, Mr Horace Templeman, had offered a prize of five pounds to the first woman who volunteered to sit alone in the deserted cinema and watch the two films – starting at midnight.

'Five quid?' said Aunt Flo. 'You wouldn't get me in there on my own for 500 quid, let alone five. Who would be daft enough to want to do that?'

Uncle Bill roared with laughter, smacking the paper with his open palm and rocking backwards and forwards in his seat.

'You'll never guess in a million years,' he said.

'Come on, Bill, you know I hate guessing,' said Aunt Flo, who could be quite short-tempered when the mood seized her.

'All right, then, I'll tell you,' said Uncle Bill, trying to get the words out between gales of laughter. 'It's her next door!'

'That doesn't surprise me at all,' said Aunt Flo. 'That Daphne Shore is daft enough to do anything.'

'And with anybody,' said Uncle Bill.

'Don't say things like that in front of the boy,' said Aunt Flo primly.

According to the story in the paper, Mr Templeman had put up a notice in the foyer of the Regal, inviting female patrons to volunteer to undertake the lonely vigil.

If the person who took on the task managed to sit through both horror films without taking flight or fright, there would be a prize of five pounds and free seats at the cinema for a month – a considerable reward for enduring three nerve-racking hours in dark isolation.

The paper's report said that, much to Mr Templeman's surprise, only one woman had offered to face the test – none other than Mrs Daphne Shore, who happened to be the next door neighbour of Aunt Flo and Uncle Bill.

Mrs Shore was notable for quite a few things, not the least of them being her huge mop of yellow hair, which sat on her rather large head like a beehive. I cannot remember anyone else with such a flamboyant hairstyle at that time. Perhaps she was a good few years ahead of the fashions without knowing it.

She wore lots of make-up, particularly lipstick, orange in colour and thickly layered. Her dresses were short and tight and the heels of her shoes were high. Not surprisingly, she walked with a bit of a wobble.

She also had a very friendly disposition, ever ready to chat with anyone, especially men. She could often be seen on her front doorstep in conversation with the milkman, the bread deliveryman or even a passing ice cream salesman. Her laugh was loud and raucous and she showed her teeth a great deal when she did so.

I remember walking home to Aunt Flo's house one night and seeing Mrs Shore standing in a darkened shop doorway with a man. It was not her husband, but it was obviously someone she knew well because they were standing very close and she appeared to be whispering in his ear.

Daphne Shore was certainly popular with the male inhabitants of the estate but was not too well regarded by the womenfolk. I could not understand this contrast in attitudes at the time.

Her husband, Harry, was a different kettle of fish. He was small, slightly built and mild of manner. Everybody liked him and felt sorry for him. He was quietly spoken and polite and it was generally agreed by all the neighbours that he was 'put upon' by his extrovert spouse. They also agreed that he was too soft for his own good.

Before he married, Mr Shore had been in the Merchant Navy and had sailed to all parts of the world. I once heard Uncle Bill say, 'I wouldn't mind betting he'd rather be on the high seas now than be here with her.'

Aunt Flo summed it all up with the verdict, 'She walks all over him,' adding as a final condemnation, 'What's more, she dresses like a slut and those front-room curtains of hers are a disgrace to the street.'

It was not the first time that Aunt Flo had made comments about those curtains, which were coloured red, green, blue and yellow and stood out like a beacon in the dull setting of Ivy Street.

Aunt Flo was a strange mixture, fussy about some things, dilatory in other matters. Like Aunt Nell, her colouring was dark and attractive, but she lacked her sister's dress sense and always looked slightly dishevelled.

Even when she was 'dolled up to go out' – one of her favourite expressions – she never appeared to have put as much effort into it as she might have done.

She held strong views, regarding most things as either black or white. There were no shades of grey. In her eyes, Mrs Shore had little to recommend her and was definitely on the black list.

As I lay in bed that night, I thought about the two horror films to be shown at the Regal and Mrs Shore's brave acceptance of the challenge to watch them alone in the small hours. A little plan of my own began to take shape.

The following day I discussed it with Norman Mason. We were sitting in the hen coop that occupied nearly half of his mother's back garden.

The structure had been erected for her by a cousin who had bought it cheap and had then discovered that his landlord would not allow him to have it on his property. Mrs Mason was now saving up to buy some pullets to occupy it, an introduction Norman and I eagerly awaited.

'I wouldn't mind seeing that Frankenstein film,' I said.

'We'd never get in,' said Norman. 'The manager would throw us out as soon as we got in the foyer.'

'Not if he didn't see us,' I said, trying to sound crafty.

'He'd see us all right. He's always hanging around the box office when they are showing horror pictures.'

'What if we sneaked in the back way the night Mrs Shore watches the films on her own?' I asked. 'No one would spot us if we did that.'

Norman, who was ever-ready for an adventure, looked intrigued, and as I outlined my plan he fell in with it readily.

It was all so simple. The midnight showing was due to be held the following Monday, after the normal evening performance. My plan was that we should slip in through the rear exit as patrons were leaving and hide in the toilets.

I was sure that no one would disturb us. After all, the only people in the cinema after the audience had gone would be Mrs Shore, the projectionist and possibly the manager, to supervise the challenge.

When we heard the soundtrack as the first film began at midnight, we could leave the toilets, crawl along the rows and find ourselves a couple of seats. It would be dark in the auditorium and there would be no one to see us, other than Mrs Shore, and she would be too busy watching the films. It was a foolproof scheme.

'What shall we tell our mams?' said Norman, again revealing his weakness for giving the game away.

'You ask your mam if I can stay with you at your house on Monday night. My mam won't mind. She knows I'll be all right at your place. Then, when your mam and gran are asleep, we can get up, dress and sneak out of the house. We shall be back before four o'clock and nobody will know we have been anywhere.'

Norman and I had carried out such a stunt once before when we had decided to go on a midnight ramble through a wood about a mile from the housing estate. It had worked perfectly then and I could see no reason why it should not succeed again.

And it did. Mrs Mason and her aged mother always went to bed early and we were able to creep out of the house without a sound.

Getting into the cinema through the rear exit was equally easy and we reached our destination, the toilets, without incident. Then came the long wait.

Voices carried in the empty cinema, and we thought we heard that of Mrs Shore. We also heard a man talking, and assumed it was the manager showing her to her seat and giving her a final reminder about the rules of the challenge.

Eventually, the opening music to *Frankenstein* began, the signal for us to get down on our hands and knees and crawl into the auditorium.

As my eyes became accustomed to the darkness, I peeped round the seat at the end of a row to see if I could spot where

Mrs Shore was sitting. She was in the centre of the ninepennies, the best seats downstairs. But she was not alone.

Sitting beside her was Mr Templeman. I knew it was him because of his shiny bald head. He had both arms around her and they appeared to be kissing. Neither of them showed the slightest interest in what was going on on the screen. I found it hard to believe that anybody would waste their time doing that when they could be watching Boris Karloff.

Curiosity got the better of Norman. Instead of turning his attention to the film, he began to crawl up the aisle in the direction of the couple, who by this time were making funny noises. I had to follow.

We approached as near as we dared in order to get a close-up view of these odd activities in the ninepennies. Suddenly Mrs Shore sat up straight and pushed Mr Templeman away.

'Now,' she said, in the firm manner in which I had heard her address her husband Harry many times. 'You're sure you have ordered the removal van for Wednesday?'

'Of course I have,' said Mr Templeman. 'It'll be there at eight o'clock.'

'It mustn't get there before then. You never know. Harry might be a bit late going to work and then the fat would be in the fire.'

'Don't fret, Daphne, it'll be all right.'

'And the van mustn't be late coming. I want us to be well on our way before Harry comes home. There could be a terrible carry-on if he catches us. You know what these quiet blokes are like when they are roused.'

'Don't worry, it's all arranged. I've never let you down, have I?'

'No, and you hadn't better start, neither.'

With that, the kissing resumed and Norman and I crawled as far away as possible so that we could watch the films with the minimum risk of being spotted.

Mr Templeman must have been acting as projectionist that night because, when *Frankenstein* ended, he went upstairs to make the change-over to *Dracula*. We kept our heads well down until he resumed his seat alongside Mrs Shore.

Just before the Bela Lugosi film drew to a close, Norman and I crawled out of the auditorium, unlocked the rear exit door, and set off for Mrs Mason's house. The cold night air made us shiver after the warmth of the cinema.

As we hurried along, I said to Norman, 'Listen, Norm, whatever you do, don't tell anybody about all this. You'll get us shot if you do.'

Norman promised that not a word would escape his lips. Like me, he recognised that, successful though our exploit had been, retribution would be swift and painful if anyone found out.

As for Mrs Shore and her liaison with Mr Templeman, the least said the better. There would be domestic ructions all round if that came out into the open, to say nothing of the fact that we might be banned from ever attending the Regal again.

Two days later, on the fateful Wednesday, I was playing a game of marbles with Norman in Aunt Flo's back garden. Mr Shore came out of his kitchen door and looked over the fence.

'Is your auntie in?' he asked. He appeared serious and even paler than usual.

When I nodded, he vaulted over the fence and tapped on the back door. Aunt Flo opened it and said, 'What's the matter, Harry? What's the trouble?'

'Would you and Bill come round for a minute? I want to show you something,' he replied.

Clearly intrigued by the request and Mr Shore's gloomy manner, Aunt Flo called over her shoulder to Uncle Bill.

'Harry wants us to pop round his house. Something's up!' she shouted.

The pair of them followed Mr Shore next door. Norman and I trailed behind them.

Mr Shore opened his front door and beckoned us in. The sight that confronted us brought a squeal of astonishment from Aunt Flo. Uncle Bill made a whistling noise and said, 'Bloody hell!'

They had good reason to be shocked. The living room was completely bare except for a small stool standing in the centre. On top of the seat were a cup and saucer, a plate, and a knife, fork and spoon.

'That's all she's left me,' said Mr Shore.

'What do you mean, Harry – that's all she's left you?' said Aunt Flo, trying to come to grips with the situation.

'Daphne. She's gone. She's run off with that bloke who manages the Regal. They've gone to Southport to live – according to that,' said Mr Shore, pointing at what was obviously a curt farewell note propped against an empty jam jar on the mantelpiece.

'But where's all the furniture?' asked Uncle Bill.

'She's taken that as well. The whole lot. Everything. The crockery, the beds, the wireless, the stair carpet. She's left me the kettle, but not the teapot.'

We looked in amazement around the room and it then dawned on us that Mrs Shore had even taken her gaudy front window curtains. Aunt Flo seemed pleased about that.

'When did all this happen?' asked Uncle Bill.

'This morning, not long after I went to work, according to her on the other side,' said Mr Shore. 'A removal van turned up, they piled everything into it, and off they went.'

'Well, at least she left you with something to sit on and something to eat with,' said Uncle Bill, trying to look on the bright side.

'That's not much comfort,' said Aunt Flo, waves of indignation sweeping over her after the initial shock.

Mr Shore led us through all the rooms in the house. Like the living room, they were bare.

'Didn't you know what was going on?' said Uncle Bill.

'I'd got no idea. I know she spent a lot of time at the pictures. Sometimes she went to see the same film twice at the Regal, but I never thought anything of it. Well, you wouldn't, would you?'

Judging by the expression on Uncle Bill's face, he certainly would have done, but he made no comment.

'What are you going to do now, Harry?' asked Aunt Flo. 'I mean, where are you going to sleep tonight? You can't sleep on the bare boards, can you?'

Mr Shore permitted himself a watery smile. 'Don't worry about that, Flo,' he said. 'I can go round and spend the night at my sister's. She'll let me have a bed.'

Norman had little to say as we walked round to his house to continue our game of marbles in his mother's hen coop. He appeared puzzled.

I felt very sad because I liked Mr Shore. Apart from anything else, he always gave me his spare cigarette cards and he never grumbled if I kicked my tennis ball into his garden.

'Poor old Mr Shore,' I said. 'I can't get over her clearing off like that and not telling him. It must have come as a bit of a shock when he got home and found she had gone.'

Norman was silent for a few seconds, and then he said, 'But he knew.'

'Knew what?'

'That Mrs Shore was going to run away with Mr Templeman.'

'How could he know if she didn't tell him?'

'Because I told him,' said Norman sheepishly.

'But you promised not to,' I said, feeling let down.

'Yes, but I couldn't stop myself. You know me.'

'I know you all right. When did you tell him?'

'I saw him coming home from work last night, so I went up to him and told him.'

'What did he say?'

'He just gave me a funny smile and said, "Really?" Then he

gave me a shilling and asked me to promise not to tell anybody else about it.'

The whole incident disturbed me for the rest of the evening, and when I got to bed it occupied my thoughts so fully that I did not drop off to sleep for hours.

If Mr Shore had been warned that his wife was going to run away, why didn't he stop her? Why didn't he confront Mr Templeman and have a showdown, as they did in all the best cowboy pictures? Perhaps the neighbours were right in the summing-up of his character. Perhaps he was too soft to stick up for himself, too scared to defend his rights.

Then the penny dropped and it all became clear. Mr Shore actually wanted her to leave. He was glad to see the back of her. And, in keeping with his nature, he was anxious that it should happen with as little fuss as possible.

As I lay in bed, with the blanket pulled up under my chin, I realised I had been given another lesson in the strange and unpredictable ways of adults, particularly the relationships between men and women.

A week later, Harry Shore rejoined the Merchant Navy. We never saw him again, but he sent Aunt Flo a postcard from Hong Kong. It contained a short but revealing message: 'Never been happier in my life. Regards, Harry.'

THE CORNER-SHOP
CASANOVAS

B EING WITHOUT a father in the Thirties had many disadvantages, not the least of them the lack of someone to boast about.

Of course, a boy in such a situation might have his mother to fall back upon, but it was not the same thing.

Much as he appreciated her love and care, when it came to talk in the school playground there was little he could say about her to his friends that would enable him to bask in reflected glory. Telling your pals that she made the best date pudding in the world cut no ice at all. Such culinary ability had no glamour or excitement attached to it. In any case, all small boys thought their mother made the finest date pudding to come out of a basin.

Equally, it was no good claiming that your mother kept you clean and reasonably well-dressed and never failed to mend the holes in your socks. Staying clean and tidy did not figure high in the priorities of any schoolboy worth his salt, and a hole in your sock was a mark of distinction, a sign that you lived life to its full, rugged potential.

Without question, a male parent was essential if you were to hold your own in the great game of one-upmanship that was played out so intensely in the communities of the young.

Few missed the opportunity to extol the abilities of their fathers, usually concerned with their physical powers or sporting talents. It did not matter too much if these claims were exaggerated. As long as they contained a grain of truth they were acceptable to most.

One boy I knew never missed the chance to tell us that his father could have played cricket for England if he had wanted to.

Now and again a sceptic in the group would say, 'Well, why didn't he then?' The answer was always the same: 'Because he had better things to do with his time.'

There was no arguing with that reply, even though we all knew that the man in question spent most of his leisure hours playing dominoes in a nearby working-men's club and was about as athletic as a lame hippopotamus.

Another boy claimed that his father had once knocked out Phil Scott, at that time a leading heavyweight boxer. If anyone asked where and when this remarkable pugilistic feat occurred, the boy would reply darkly: 'Never you mind.'

The fact that the boy's father weighed only about nine stones even when wearing his overcoat and heavy boots did not detract too much from the validity of the story.

If such outrageous boasting was original enough, it was good enough for the schoolboy fraternity. Once a tale was told, the hunt would be on for a claim to top it.

In the main, boasts were generally built around a father's native strength. Consequently, when boys quarrelled and the argument reached stalemate, it was the regular practice to break off the engagement with the classic words: 'Anyway, I bet my dad could bash your dad any day.'

Not surprisingly, with all the claims and counter-claims flying around the playgrounds and at street corners, the boy without a father was at a considerable disadvantage. He had no one to put up as a hero. It was no use singing the praises of a brawny uncle or a tough older cousin. Such relatives did not count.

For these reasons, among many others, I often wished I had a father. I longed for the chance to praise his abilities and sometimes would form a mental picture of the ideal parent. He would be tall and muscular, with a jaunty walk and a positive air. He would be something like the film actor, Gary Cooper, but even bigger.

It might have been my desire to play a more leading role in the councils of my schoolboy peers that prompted me to attempt to play Cupid on behalf of my widowed mother.

It was a well-intentioned effort, but, like so many of my childhood schemes, it did not work out the way I had planned it. Even so, it was not the disaster it might have been.

It so happened that, indirectly, King George V and Queen Mary played a part in the venture, which eventually provided a turning point in my life and that of my long-suffering mother.

It also brought my one and only close encounter with the much-feared Pikey Hull. A human monster if ever there was one, Pikey, the terror of young and old alike, was to figure prominently in the drama. More of him later.

The story began not long after we had moved from Aunt Flo's house to take up temporary residence at the home of Aunt Maud and Uncle Jack.

Like Aunt Flo, they had a council house on the Mill Farm estate, but it was in an area some distance from Ivy Street and close to the old part of the town. The local council must have been going through a literary phase at the time because all the streets in this neighbourhood were named after poets. The one in which Aunt Maud and Uncle Jack lived was called Wordsworth Street.

Our departure from Aunt Flo's house was not the result of some unpleasant family squabble. It followed a normal routine, because our switch from one set of relatives to another was as natural as night following day.

All five aunts and their husbands were happy to take it in turns to provide my mother and me with a roof over our heads. The unwritten rule was that each stay should be limited to a few months and that the next in line to play hosts should make the offer of accommodation before the current providers of hospitality had become fed up with our presence.

The arrangement was fair; no one abused the system, and, in the main, everybody was happy with it. We had moved around so much over the last two or three years that one set of lodgings became much like another as far as I was concerned, but I must confess that I had my favourites among the five on the rota.

Least favourite for me was the home of Aunt Maud and Uncle Jack. It was a well-run household because Aunt Maud was a very fussy woman who put cleanliness above all else.

I always had to take my shoes off before crossing the threshhold, even if they were as clean as a whistle, and we all had to wash our hands so often that it seemed there was never a time when there was not a small queue at the kitchen sink.

Aunt Maud's pride and joy was a three-piece suite, which dominated the small, dust-free living room, or lounge, as she preferred to call it. I was allowed the luxury of sitting on the chairs and the settee, but Aunt Maud used to spread three sheets of newspaper on the seat before I did so.

'You never know, Madge,' she used to say to my mother. 'You know what boys are like for wetting themselves and it's better to be safe than sorry.'

Aunt Maud was the smallest of the five aunts, but that did not exactly put her in the lightweight division. She had sharp features and a faintly dyspeptic look that fitted her rather gloomy outlook on life.

Fond of sayings and proverbs, she had one for any kind of situation. If her husband burped in company after a heavy meal, she would hide her embarrassment with the words 'Better out than in'. If anyone did anything out of character, she would remind us that we should 'never judge a leopard by its spots'. And if she ever suspected someone of not being all they claimed to be, she would warn us that 'a book should not be judged by its cover'.

There were dozens like these in her repertoire, many of them so obscure they hardly made sense within the context of the conversation. The one that puzzled my young mind the most was that which she used whenever the fates appeared to be unkind. 'God does not pay his debts with money,' she would say whenever anyone complained about life's injustices.

Uncle Jack was a nice man. He was usually very quiet, except when in the company of ladies, when he used to talk a lot and flash his extremely white teeth at every opportunity. He was something of a dandy, although I could never understand why he regularly wore an artificial white scarf instead of a collar and tie. I would not have been surprised to learn that he went to bed in it.

My ever-present yearning for a hero figure of my very own grew stronger during our stay with Aunt Maud, and it took on almost unbearable proportions one wet Saturday morning when a crowd of us stood outside the Kipling Street fish and chip shop, enjoying the heady aroma that wafted out so tantalisingly from that much-used establishment.

We had been joined by a newcomer to the district whose undistinguished appearance and mild manner had automatically placed him well down the gang's pecking order. At least that was the situation until he reached into the back pocket of his trousers and produced an old newspaper cutting.

The piece of paper, which was beginning to come apart at the creases, showed a team of footballers, their hair plastered down, their arms folded, and their faces uniformly set in a grim expression as though they were awaiting a firing squad.

The caption revealed that the players were members of the Tranmere Rovers team of several seasons earlier and it listed their names in the traditional left to right order.

There was nothing special about the photograph – we had all seen dozens like it – but that changed when the new boy, whose name was Bobby Candlish, announced, somewhat diffidently, that the man third from the left in the front row was none other than his father, Jackie Candlish, a centre-forward who had once been included in a set of cigarette cards depicting noted soccer players of the era.

We were stunned into silence. It was such an impressive claim that no one had the nerve to cast doubts on its authenticity.

Bobby threw in the extra information that his father had had to give up football because of injury and had just taken up a job as a salesman for one of the town's boot and shoe companies.

One or two members of the gang made half-hearted attempts to say that their fathers nearly got trials for Aston Villa or Bolton Wanderers, but they were forlorn and pathetic bids to steal Bobby Candlish's thunder.

No matter how we tried to look at it, there was no arguing that Bobby was now the top dog when it came to having a hero for a father.

As for me, I was a complete also-ran. I had nobody, not even someone I could lie about. I made up my mind, there and then, that I had to do something about it. I had to get a father from somewhere.

As I lay in bed that night, pondering on the problem, I began to realise that the task might not be as difficult as it looked on the surface.

Even at that tender age, I was aware that obtaining a husband for my mother was not like buying a suit off the peg at the Fifty Shilling Tailors.

The man selected for the job had to be interested in the first place, and here I was in luck. There were two candidates, both of whom had made it plain in various ways that they had a warm spot for my mother. By a remarkable coincidence, both were shopkeepers, but the similarity ended there.

Their corner shops were situated in streets of privately owned houses in the old part of the town, just off Wordsworth Street.

The one owned by Bill Clarke was a proper store, with two large show windows and plenty of room on the pavement for displaying fruit and vegetables.

The other, belonging to Fred Starling, was an improvised affair, with the goods for sale stacked high in what used to be the front room of his house.

Mr Clarke had two wide counters, on one of which stood a gleaming bacon slicer and a cash register that tinkled every time its buttons were pressed.

Mr Starling had only a small counter and kept his takings in a shoe box balanced on top of a sweet jar. He did not own a bacon slicer, but he did have a lethal-looking carving knife which he used with some skill, although the thickness of his bacon varied considerably from slice to slice.

For all its technical advantages, Mr Clarke's establishment did not compare with Mr Starling's little store when it came to colour and atmosphere. The latter's shop had character, but, more importantly, its owner was a nicer, kinder man than Mr Clarke.

On top of all that, Fred Starling was more honest than his rival in the nearby street. This honesty and fairness revealed itself in all sorts of ways. For example, Mr Starling would never dream of giving a customer short weight. If, say, he was bagging up a pound of carrots, he would cut a vegetable in half to make sure the purchaser received the exact amount.

Mr Clarke, on the other hand, was not above pressing a finger on the scales to tilt things in his favour. I saw him do this dozens of times and it offended my schoolboy sense of fair play.

The two shopkeepers differed in so many ways, even in their approaches to my mother. Mr Starling was always polite, picking his words carefully so as not to appear too forward. If their fingers brushed when he handed my mother her change, he would take his hand away quickly and look embarrassed.

Mr Clarke went to the opposite extreme. He was full of quips and jokes. I did not understand half the things he said to my mother, but they were punctuated by broad winks and smirking smiles. On more than one occasion my mother told him not to be so saucy. And when he passed over change, he would take hold of my mother's hand and she had to pull hard to free herself.

The two men, both widowers, were also very different in appearance. Mr Clarke was fat and red faced. He always wore a natty peaked cap, a tweed jacket and a yellow pullover.

Mr Starling was pale, thin and slow moving. He wore slate-grey overalls, exactly the same colour as his closely cropped hair, which was massed on his head like iron filings congregating on a magnet.

Sometimes when I went to Mr Starling's shop to fetch things for my mother, he would take a packet of Woodbines off the shelf and discreetly slip it into the shopping bag.

'Just a little present for your mam,' he would whisper.

Mr Clarke could never be discreet. Every gesture had to be flamboyant. Now and again he would cut off a few pieces of bacon with his automatic slicer, wrap them in a sheet of grease-proof paper, and toss the package across the counter.

'Give that to your mam with my compliments,' he would say in a loud voice, following up with a wink for the benefit of any men who happened to be in the shop.

I did not like Mr Clarke very much, but Mr Starling met with my full approval. The latter was my choice for a new father. The question was: Would my mother be prepared to accept him as a new husband?

I knew she got on well with him and had a great deal of respect for his good manners and courteous behaviour. However, through listening to the conversations of grown-ups, I gathered that, although women had a high regard for such qualities as those exhibited by Mr Starling, they expected far more than this from a would-be husband.

Looking back, I can recall only one incident where my mother fell out with Mr Starling. He was in her bad books for several days, although I felt at the time that she was a bit hard on him.

It all started one Friday evening – pay night. My mother came home from the factory, gave Aunt Maud her token contribution for our food and accommodation, and then sent me to Mr Starling's shop for our usual weekend treat.

This consisted of a packet of ten Woodbines and two whipped cream walnuts (one each, which we always saved to eat in bed). I was also instructed to buy a twopenny bottle of olive oil, my weekly 'medicine', which my mother swore warded off every illness from TB to lockjaw.

The miniature bottles were roughly the size of laboratory test tubes and were tightly corked. They were attached by elasticated string to a large card hanging on one of the walls.

In fact, the wall was covered with similar cards holding small bottles containing all kinds of sticky liquids, ranging from cough syrup to hair oil.

Mr Starling's little store was crowded when I made my purchases and he was flustered. Nevertheless, he found time to ask after my mother's health and send her his best wishes.

That night we retired to our bedroom and sat side by side on my mother's bed to eat our whipped cream walnuts. It was a magical quarter of an hour as we made them last as long as we could.

Then I climbed into my camp bed in the corner and began to doze off while my mother smoked one of her Woodbines, put her hair in paper curlers, and read the Ethel M. Dell romance she had borrowed from the travelling library. Eventually my mother put out the light and I began to settle down for a deep sleep.

'Have you taken your olive oil?' came my mother's voice from the darkness.

I sat up with a jerk. Not for the first time, I had forgotten.

'Drink it now, there's a good boy,' she said.

I reached under the camp bed, found the bottle, pulled out the cork and gulped down the contents.

'Have you drunk it all?'

'Yes, mam.'

'Good boy. You'll never be poorly while you drink your olive oil.'

An hour later I awoke with a start and was violently sick all over the bedclothes. My mother panicked on occasions like this and she scuttled along the landing to fetch Aunt Maud and Uncle Jack. They stumbled after her as she hurried back to our room and the three of them stood looking down at me.

'He's as white as a sheet,' said my mother. 'Is he sickening for something, Maud?'

'There's never smoke without fire,' said Aunt Maud, who was able to dredge up one of her pet sayings whatever the situation.

I lay still, fearful that any movement would launch another wave of sickness. My mother, so stoic in most things, could not cope with illness of any sort, mainly because she managed to convince herself that death was the inevitable conclusion of even the slightest ailment.

Even so, it made us all jump when she put her hands on either side of her face and let out a piercing scream.

'Look – it's green,' she shouted.

'What's green?' asked Uncle Jack, now fully awake, thanks to the scream.

'That stuff,' said my mother, pointing to the mess on the eiderdown. She was right. The colour was bright green.

'He's got gangrene from somewhere,' said Aunt Maud, ever the pessimist.

'Don't talk daft,' said Uncle Jack as my mother began to cry, fearing the worst, as usual.

At that moment Uncle Jack spotted the miniature bottle lying on the floor beside my bed.

'What's this?' he said, bending to pick it up.

'That's his olive oil. You know he has it every week,' said my mother.

Uncle Jack read the label glued around the bottle and looked up in triumph, like a detective in the films who has just solved a difficult case.

'This isn't an olive oil bottle,' he said. 'This bottle had hair oil in it. Ronnie's drunk a bottle of hair oil. No wonder he's been sick. No wonder it's green.'

My mother stopped crying at once. Anger took over – and it was directed at Mr Starling.

'Fancy him giving him hair oil instead of olive oil,' she howled. 'I'll be round there tomorrow morning to tell him what I think of him. He could have killed our Ronnie with that stuff.'

'He was ever so busy when I went to the shop,' I croaked, desperately trying to defend Mr Starling.

'I don't care how busy he was,' said my mother, stoking up her fury. 'He had no right to give you hair oil. It could have been poisonous.'

Fortunately for Mr Starling, by the following morning my mother's anger had subsided, but still she gave him what she called 'a piece of her mind'. A few days went by before she took her custom back to the shop and they resumed their gentle friendship.

Having decided that Mr Starling should be my new father, I turned my attention to eliminating the other suitor from the contest.

I knew it would not be easy. Mr Clarke had a far more positive approach to wooing, and in the normal course of events the reticent Mr Starling would not stand a chance. Somehow I had to tilt the odds in the latter's favour.

It was at this stage in the story that the awful Pikey Hull arrived on the scene, although I have to admit that involving him in my plan was done on the spur of the moment.

Pikey Hull was heartily disliked by everyone in Wordsworth Street, mainly because everybody was frightened of him – children and grown-ups alike. Pikey was an aggressive bully, ready to fight anyone who earned his slightest displeasure. He was not very tall but he was solidly built, with wide shoulders and forearms like Popeye. He did not wash very often and he wore a perpetual scowl.

He had four children, all of whom were scared of him. His wife, a docile, spiritless woman, was frequently on the receiving end of his flailing fists and as a result seemed to have a permanent black eye and cut lips.

The Hull children often had nasty red weals on the backs of their legs, the outcome of Pikey's ready use of the thick, buckled belt he wore. Even other people's children were not safe from Pikey. He would clip their ears on the slightest pretext, and the sad thing was that there was not a father in the street brave enough to stop him.

The male inhabitants of Wordsworth Street were a disappointment to me, especially as some of them had been courageous enough to withstand the rigours of Western Front trench life during the Great War.

I came to the depressing conclusion that German machine-gun nests and heavy-artillery fire held fewer terrors for them than Pikey Hull's granite fists. It was not surprising, then, that this monstrous man reigned supreme in our area of the council estate.

The day that Pikey became involved in my life, my mother

had instructed me to call at Mr Clarke's shop on my way home from school to pick up a quarter of potted meat for our tea.

As usual, Mr Clarke was cracking jokes and whistling snatches of popular songs as he served, and, as usual, he generated much laughter among his customers. I made a point of staying stony-faced.

Before handing over the paper bag containing the potted meat, Mr Clarke said, 'Hang on a minute.'

He took a piece of paper from under the counter, scribbled on it, folded it twice, and pushed it into my hand.

'Give that to your mam for me,' he said. 'And don't lose it on the way home.'

As I set off along Wordsworth street I could not resist the temptation. I unfolded the paper and read its contents: 'Dear Madge, would you like to come to the pictures with me on Friday, love Billy Boy.'

I was appalled by the prospect, so much so that I did not look where I was going and bumped into Pikey Hull as he was about to slouch through the wooden gate leading into his small front garden.

True to character, Pikey grabbed me by the ear and gave it a vicious pull that lifted me onto my toes.

'Why don't you look what you're doing?' he growled.

'Sorry, Mr Hull,' I bleated. Even as I uttered the apology, a plan leapt into my mind. It was built around the simple but vital fact that Pikey's wife and my mother shared the same Christian name – Madge.

'Mr Clarke down at the shop asked me to give this to Mrs Hull,' I said, holding up the note.

Pikey snatched it from my hand and read it, his lips forming the words as he did so. His rage was terrible to behold and a torrent of swear words could be heard all along the street. He gave me such a violent push that I fell into the road, hitting my head on a drain cover. Still swearing, he marched off in the direction of Mr Clarke's shop.

Forgetting the pain from my bruised head and twisted ear, I ran after him, terrified by the spectacle of the demon I had unleashed and fearful of the consequences.

When he reached the shop, Pikey flung open the door, strode in, grasped the unsuspecting Mr Clarke by the collars of his tweed jacket, and pulled him halfway across the counter.

Pressing his face close to that of the startled shopkeeper, Pikey bellowed, 'You keep away from my Madge. She belongs to me and nobody else, especially a little twerp like you. If I catch you as much as looking at her again I will smash you to pieces – and your bleeding shop. Have you got that?'

'Sorry, Mr Hull,' spluttered the hapless Mr Clarke. 'I didn't know.'

'Well, you bloody well know now,' said Pikey, pushing the shopkeeper so hard that he fell against the shelves behind the counter, dislodging several tins of corned beef.

I had been peeping round the door to watch the confrontation, but ran off at speed as soon as Pikey turned to leave.

As I made my way back to Aunt Maud's house by a devious route, still clutching our quarter of potted meat, I could not help but entertain a feeling of satisfaction. My off-the-cuff scheme had worked out admirably.

It was clear that Mr Clarke thought Pikey was referring to my mother, thinking she was his 'fancy woman', and would therefore keep his distance in future. No one had been hurt in the process – except me – and the way was now open for Mr Starling to pursue his wooing without a rival. Not for the first time, I was wrong.

The following Saturday my mother appeared to be on edge – not in an irritable, nervy way, but pleasantly excited as though in anticipation of something.

I was even more puzzled when she announced that she had an

appointment at the hairdressers. This was a rare event because she usually did her own hair, not being able to afford regular visits to a salon.

Aunt Maud also seemed brighter – almost cheerful, in fact. She spent a lot of time making a trifle and fetched down her best china tea service from the top shelf in the kitchen cupboard. It dawned on me that something was afoot, confirmation coming after the midday meal when Uncle Jack abandoned his silk scarf and put on a collar and tie. My mother explained it all when she returned from the hairdressers.

'There's somebody coming for tea,' she said as she helped me to button up my best white shirt and put a Windsor knot in my tie. 'Now, you'll be a good boy, won't you? You won't let me down, will you?'

The visitor arrived on the stroke of four o'clock. He was of medium height, but strongly built, and he wore a navy blue three-piece suit that was beginning to develop a shine. His white cloth cap was set at a jaunty angle, but he took it off and stuffed it into his pocket as my mother introduced him to Aunt Maud and Uncle Jack on the doorstep.

My mother, wearing more lipstick and rouge than I had ever seen her use before, was almost twinkling with pleasure. After the grown-up formalities had been concluded, she drew me to her, put her hands on my shoulders, and said with a dazzling smile, 'And this is my Ronnie. Ronnie, I would like you to meet my new friend, Ray.'

'Hello, Ronnie,' said the man. There was a faint drawl to his voice and I learned later that he had spent the previous five years on a farm in Canada.

He took my hand in his and shook it vigorously, just as though I had adult status. I appreciated the gesture. Then he reached into his pocket and drew out a small but well-filled paper bag.

'You like soldiers, don't you?' he said, handing me the bag.

I opened it and looked inside. It contained about ten lead soldiers in Grenadier Guards' uniforms and carrying rifles as though on parade. He must have gone to the trouble to go to Woolworth's to buy them for me.

As far as I was concerned, it was a marvellous start to the visit, and the tea itself proved equally agreeable. Aunt Maud invited Ray to take off his jacket as we sat down at the table and we all enjoyed tinned-salmon salad and the rich trifle that followed.

My mother fussed over the visitor from start to finish, jumping up every few minutes to make sure his teacup was full. Uncle Jack and Ray found a common interest in boxing and they talked non-stop about the great fighters of the day. Throughout it all Aunt Maud smiled knowingly every time she caught my mother's eye.

Towards the end of the meal Ray saw me looking at a red and blue mark showing below the cuff of his right sleeve.

'Do you know what that is?' he asked.

I shook my head.

'It's a tattoo,' he said, rolling up his sleeve to show a snake entwined round a dagger. The tattoo occupied the whole of his forearm from elbow to wrist. He then rolled up his other sleeve to reveal an identical tattoo on his left arm.

Aunt Maud did not look too impressed, but my mother obviously approved of them. 'I think they are pretty and colourful,' she said. No one disagreed with her.

Later on, Ray took my mother into the town for a drink in one of the pubs. I stayed with Aunt Maud and Uncle Jack and I heard them talking as they did the washing up in the kitchen.

'He'll be all right for our Madge, don't you think, Jack?' said Aunt Maud.

'Course he will,' said Uncle Jack. 'Seems like a nice bloke to me.'

'You can see he likes the boy. Do you think he will be good to him? He won't knock him about, will he?'

'Course he won't knock him about. He'll make a good father.'

So there it was – a ready-made dad on the way with no help whatsoever from me. But much as I appreciated the gift of the lead soldiers, Ray did not quite match up to Mr Starling in my eyes. The quiet shopkeeper was still my favourite.

Little did I know then that there would be an incident on the day of the forthcoming Silver Jubilee of King George V and Queen Mary that would alter my views completely.

Like most streets in most towns and villages throughout the country, the residents of Wordsworth Street had been planning a Jubilee party for the children.

The women had pooled their limited food resources in order to make sure that the youngsters had a spread that did justice to the royal occasion and kitchen tables were brought out to make one long festive board in the middle of the road.

The men had clubbed together to buy a few crates of light ale so that the grown-ups could join in the celebrations; sprint and relay races had been planned for all age groups, and there would also be a fancy dress competition and a talent contest.

No doubt about it, the people of Wordsworth Street intended to rise above their domestic, financial and social problems and mark their monarch's anniversary with as much style as they could muster.

The street was a hive of activity early in the morning of the big day, most residents being occupied with the job of draping colourful home-made bunting across the fronts of their houses.

There were frequent conferences as last-minute plans were made and much coming and going between houses as plates of cakes and bowls of jellies were brought out for inspection and approval.

The children of the street could hardly contain their excitement as they watched the preparations, and they raised a cheer when one of the men, Mr Bradbury from number 33, unfurled a large Union Jack flag.

'Where shall we fly it?' he asked his fellow committee members.

They pondered for a few seconds and then one of them said, 'Well, there's only one place for it – right at the top of The Pole.'

He was speaking of a thirty-feet tall, cast iron column that arose from the pavement not far from Aunt Maud's house. No one knew for certain exactly what purpose it served, but it was generally considered that it was used to disperse excessive gases that built up in the sewer system. Residents simply referred to it as 'The Pole' and left it at that.

'Nobody's got a ladder long enough to reach the top of that,' said Mr Bradbury. 'Somebody will have to shin up it if we want it to fly right at the top.'

Everybody agreed that the Union Jack should flutter from the highest possible point in the street and immediately one of the younger men volunteered to make the climb.

He got off to a good start, wrapping his legs around the thick rust-riddled pole and lifting himself up a few inches at a time. He managed to climb six or seven feet, but by then it could be seen that he did not have the strength to get any higher. He clung on for a couple of minutes but eventually slid back to the ground and admitted, somewhat sheepishly, that the task was beyond him.

By this time practically every resident of Wordsworth Street had gathered around the pole, keen to see who could conquer this local Everest.

Encouraged by their wives and offspring, half a dozen more men made the attempt, but, like the first volunteer, they did not get far, sliding back to the pavement to sympathetic rounds of applause.

It was at this point that Pikey Hull pushed his way through the crowd and stood glaring at Mr Bradbury.

'Give us that flag,' he muttered. 'I'll put the bloody thing up.'

There was absolute silence as Pikey started his climb. I was keen to see the Union Jack flying at the very top but I did not want Pikey to have the glory of achieving the feat. I suspected that most people in the crowd felt the same way.

With his arms and legs wrapped firmly round the pole, Pikey began to edge higher and higher, grunting and cursing every inch of the way.

He was about 12 or 14 feet up when he came to a stop. We could hear him breathing heavily and could see that he was struggling to hold on, never mind rising any higher. There was not a sound from the crowd as they watched. Then, slowly but surely, Pikey began to slide down the pole, eventually falling in a crumpled heap at its base.

It was the signal for a loud burst of laughter from the crowd. Pikey's humiliation was complete. It really was a case of the mighty fallen. He picked himself up, muttered a few more oaths, pushed his way through the crowd, and retreated to his house.

Looking round, I noticed my mother standing with Ray at the back. She leaned close to him and whispered in his ear. He nodded and came to the front of the crowd.

'I'll have a try, if you like,' he said quietly.

He took the flag and tucked a corner of it in his belt. After a quick glance at my mother, he curled his legs around the column and began to shin skywards. Without pause, and at surprising speed, he reached the top, gripping the pole with his knees while he tied the Union Jack in place. It was a masterly performance.

As he completed the operation, there was a spontaneous burst of applause from the crowd, followed by a rousing cheer. I was so filled with pride that I could not resist the lie.

'That's my dad,' I announced to the children gathered near me.

'No he's not,' said a knowing girl with a runny nose. 'He's your mam's fancy man. I heard my gran say so.'

I refused to be defeated. 'He will be my dad – one day,' I replied.

I turned my attention to the top of the pole. Ray was grinning with satisfaction, obviously savouring the moment. He looked down at my mother, flipped the peak of his white cloth cap with the tips of his fingers, and blew her a kiss. She put both hands to her mouth and blew him a double one in return.

Ray then made a searching look around the crowd until he spotted me. He gave me a cheery wave and even at that distance I could see that it was accompanied by an elaborate wink.

My day was made, regardless of what joys lay in store during the remainder of the Silver Jubilee celebrations. Pikey Hull had been vanquished and, like the kings of medieval times, I now had my own champion who I knew would fight for me at all times, regardless of the odds. For the first time ever, I had a hero I could boast about to all my friends. King George V himself could not have been happier on that glorious day.

THE BIG BREAK-OUT
FROM ST MARY'S

S T MARY'S INFANTS and Junior School was more than a
place of learning. It was another home, a cosy haven, stiff
with discipline but warm and comforting.

There were many rules and they all had to be obeyed to the
letter. These showed clearly where you stood in the order of
things but, in turn, created a reassuring feeling of safety and
security. You knew, instinctively, that you could not come to
much harm within its walls.

The cloakroom and wash basins area reeked of carbolic
soap, the small, crowded classrooms were never free of the
faint aroma of youthful sweat, and the wooden, knot-ridden
floors were full of splinters and protruding nail heads, ever
ready to nick the kneecaps of boisterous pupils who stumbled
and fell.

We were packed like sardines when we gathered each morning for prayers in the cramped space that passed as an assembly
hall, and we did as we were told by our teachers with the speed
and precision of Grenadier Guardsmen.

Even in the playground, a large, sloping square of concrete,
surrounded by high walls, we were never free of the watchful
eye of the duty teacher, who stood, whistle in hand, prepared to
pounce on any juvenile misdemeanour in the making.

These ten-minute breaks for recreation, every morning and
afternoon, come rain or shine, followed the same pattern. The

99

girls, who giggled a lot, skipped and played hopscotch; the boys indulged in informal games of football and cricket, using coats and scarves as goalposts and chalking wickets on the crumbling walls.

The matches usually involved 20 or 30 boys each side, and the standard of sportsmanship was high, with cheating of any sort virtually unknown. If a goal was scored, no one on the other side disputed it. If a batsman missed the ball and it struck within the chalk lines of the stumps, he immediately walked off and handed the bat to the next player.

No matter how much we were enjoying our activities, the moment the teacher blew the whistle for re-assembly, the playing ceased and we raced to get into our class lines, ready to be marched back like soldiers to our studies.

There were two male teachers – the headmaster and his deputy – and both were local men. The rest were women – all spinsters, as they had to be in those days. Married women teachers were not allowed under any circumstances.

My Uncle Jack always used to say that the majority of women teachers were people whose boyfriends and fiancés had been killed in the Great War. The loss of their loved ones, he said, turned their attention to other things and many of them devoted the rest of their working lives to educating the young as a solace for not having children of their own.

I heard Uncle Jack make that observation on numerous occasions, without fully understanding exactly what he meant. But later on in life it dawned on me that perhaps that explained why women teachers could be so crabby and hard-hearted one day, loving, understanding and sympathetic the next. In fact, like most mothers.

Luckily for me, my early years of schooling were spent at St Mary's, which was surprising considering that I lived in various parts of the town during that time, sometimes quite a distance from the school.

In that era you went to the school nearest your home, and it remains a mystery how I escaped the bureaucratic net for so long. It was a piece of good fortune for which I shall be ever grateful.

My anxiety to learn, and my thirst for knowledge, sprang initially from some comments made by Grandma Perkins, my mother's mother.

Grandma Perkins (I never did know her Christian name, although I suspect it was Eliza) was a little, thin woman who always wore black. She looked pale and drawn and was constantly ill, which may explain why my mother and I did not live at her house very often during our nomadic years. I believe that my aunts decided among themselves that Grandma Perkins was not well enough to cope with a temperamental widowed daughter and a lively grandson.

Still, she always made us welcome whenever we visited for the day, although she seldom smiled to show her pleasure at our presence and said very little.

Grandpa Perkins was even less communicative. He was short and fat, wore a heavy watch-chain across his ample middle and never went out without putting on a stiff, white wing collar and a bowler hat.

He was an avid reader, as befits what was called 'an educated man' in those days. He originated from London and claimed to be a Cockney. He certainly had a funny accent, despite his years in the Midlands, and peppered what little he had to say with his favourite adjective, 'bleedin'!'

A retired factory foreman, he treated my grandma as though she was one of his female machinists. In the evenings they would sit side by side at the kitchen table, eating bread and cheese and drinking beer poured from a big white jug.

Like many of the older men of the neighbourhood, Grandpa Perkins used to fetch his ale from what was known as an 'outdoor beerhouse', but now referred to, less colourfully, as an 'off-licence'.

101

I used to enjoy watching the men, complete with their jugs, heading for the beerhouse run by a bad-tempered man named Ebenezer Holtman, on the corner of Albert Street. Most of them were fetching the drink for their wives as well as themselves, and, sad to say, some of them used to cheat – including Grandpa Perkins.

They would have their jugs filled with draught beer by the ever-acidic Ebenezer, walk out to a nearby passageway, and take massive gulps of the ale, wiping the tell-tale froth off their moustaches with the backs of their hands.

After consuming half or two-thirds of the jug's contents, depending on their thirst or greed, they would return to the shop and have it filled to the brim again. I am sure that many of the wives knew what went on, but they kept quiet in order to preserve the peace.

So Grandpa and Grandma Perkins passed their evenings, eating their bread and cheese and supping their beer out of tea cups. The only difference between them was that Grandpa always had a book in his hand and read until it was time to go to bed, hardly speaking a word from start to finish.

Grandma would occasionally mend a pair of socks or do a little knitting, but most of the time she sat bolt upright in her hard wooden chair and gazed into space, deep in thought. Grandma could not read or write and as a result was completely separated from her literature-loving husband, as though a mental steel barrier came between them in that gloomy house.

I often wondered what she was thinking about during the long evenings of silence. Was she recalling the days when, barely 13, she served as a scullery maid in a well-to-do house in south London? Her only communication with her parents in a Northamptonshire village were the letters that a son of the house wrote once a fortnight at her hesitant dictation.

Was she embittered at missing the joys of reading and

writing? Did she resent the fact that her self-centred husband had access to a world from which she had been barred all her life?

If she did entertain such feelings, she never showed them by word or deed. Her acceptance of her meagre lot was both noble and pathetic.

My mother and I were having tea at Grandma Perkins' house one wet afternoon not long after I had moved upstairs from the infants to the juniors at St Mary's.

I must have been talking about the move, because Grandma Perkins, who had hardly spoken since we arrived, suddenly put her arm round me and said, 'Make sure this boy gets a good learning, our Madge. He'll be no good unless he's learned right. If you want him to have a decent goings-on later on, you've got to see he does well at school. You don't want him to end up like me, do you?'

It was the first time I had heard even the hint of a word of self-pity from this poor, dear woman, who so seldom showed emotion or affection.

But it was the spur I needed to take schooling seriously and St Mary's to my heart. It was the start of a love affair with knowledge that hardly wavered over the next few years.

Most of the pupils at St Mary's discovered early on that all the teachers had their favourites, usually those children who showed a flair for subjects in which they themselves were particularly interested, but, in the main, they were scrupulously fair and every child was given the opportunity to learn and develop.

The two men teachers at St Mary's were more concerned with efficient administration within the building than with the skills of teaching. They ruled with an iron hand, but in entirely different ways.

Mr Waterson, the headmaster, was a firm disciplinarian with a curt manner and a military approach to everything, as befitted a former army captain who had served with distinction in the Great War. Seeing this tall, erect figure striding towards him was enough to make even the most unwilling pupil fall into line.

Mr Blyth, his deputy, was equally hard and uncompromising, but his form of discipline was based on a cruel line in sarcasm. If a pupil fell foul of Mr Blyth, through academic ignorance or bad behaviour, the teacher, with the use of a few biting words, would turn him into a laughing stock in front of his classmates.

Mr Blyth was a heavily-built man with black, curly hair, a blue-coloured chin that always looked in need of a shave, and a Charlie Chaplin moustache that seemed inappropriate on his large expanse of face.

He was a great chalk thrower and could pick out his victims with unerring accuracy. Sometimes he would have his back to the class and would be writing on the blackboard when he would sense that something untoward was going on at the rear of the form. He would swing round and, without appearing to take aim, hurl his piece of chalk in the direction of the miscreant, invariably hitting him on the chest or the head.

To be bombarded in this way by Mr Blyth was considered a distinction by the more adventurous boys, but it was a miracle that eyes were not lost during the years the deputy head practised this violent form of classroom retribution.

I did not get on too well with Mr Blyth. He always found me to be an easy target for his sarcasm and he embarrassed me a great deal.

If Mr Blyth was my least favourite teacher at St Mary's, Miss Morgan was, without doubt, my favourite. She was the Form 2b mistress and she took an interest in me from the moment I told her, quite truthfully, that I liked poetry.

What I did not tell her was that I liked going to the cinema even more, especially to see prison escape dramas starring the likes of George Raft or Paul Muni, which were all the rage at the time. If she had known about that, she might have been less kindly disposed towards me.

Despite her fierce, unsmiling countenance and apparent stony outlook on life, Miss Morgan was a romantic at heart and poetry was her true love. She always carried a small book of poems in her handbag and would write lines by Rupert Brooke or Shelley on the blackboard and encourage her class to memorise then.

Mr Blyth and Miss Morgan constituted the two extremes of schooling for me, yet, strangely, both had a role to play in the incident that nearly cost me my place at my beloved St Mary's.

At the time, my mother and I were staying with Aunt Elsie and Uncle Ted in Granville Street. It had been a fairly peaceful period in our unpredictable lives but all this was shattered one sunny afternoon in early summer.

It all started, harmlessly enough, with a few verses of a poem that Miss Morgan decided to recite to us in the middle of a geography lesson. One minute she was telling us about the barren wastes of the Sahara Desert, the next she was speaking verses telling of the joys of England on an idyllic spring day.

As always when Miss Morgan was in full recitative flow, her normally hard features took on a softer, gentler look and she tilted her head and gazed up at the ceiling.

The class, as a body, was puzzled by the sudden switch from geography to poetry, but we enjoyed listening to her musical voice.

'Did you enjoy that, children?' she asked at the conclusion.

'Yes, miss,' we chorused.

'Can anyone tell me who wrote that beautiful poem?'

There was silence for several seconds. We had not expected such a test and it took us all by surprise, especially me, because I had no idea who had penned it.

105

Eventually a hand shot up and one of the girls suggested Tennyson, but she was wrong. Another offered Coleridge and a third put forward Masefield.

The names of poets were being blurted out in a cascade – Whitman, Longfellow, Browning, Keats. With each wrong answer Miss Morgan became angrier. She was acutely disappointed and had obviously hoped for better things from us.

'Surely one of you knows who wrote that lovely poem,' she said, almost pleadingly. She turned and looked at me.

'Do you know, Ronnie?' she said.

I could see that she was praying that I would not let her down. After all, I had told her that I was very fond of poetry. Now the time had come to produce some proof of that liking.

My mind was racing in a bid to get out of the predicament, save my face and restore Miss Morgan's faith in the young in general and me in particular.

Just as I was about to admit my ignorance, it struck me that my fellow pupils had named every well-known poet except one – William Wordsworth. It was worth a guess.

'Wordsworth,' I said.

Miss Morgan permitted herself one of her rare smiles. She looked round the class and waved her arm in my direction.

'Now here's a boy who knows and loves his poetry,' she said. 'Here's a boy who will go far. He's set you all a good example. Well done, Ronnie.'

For at least five minutes I was overcome by a feeling of utter smugness, but a sense of shame replaced it. I knew I had taken the credit for something to which I was not entitled. Worse still, I had deceived Miss Morgan.

I paid little attention to the remainder of the geography lesson as I wrestled with my conscience, and when the bell sounded I walked towards Miss Morgan's desk in order to tell her that the answer I had given was only a calculated guess. Sad to say, much as I wanted to cleanse my soul, my courage failed me and I turned and followed my classmates down the stairs and into the playground.

I was still thinking about my act of deception when I walked out of the school gates and headed along Fuller Street in the direction of Aunt Elsie's house. I hoped there would be something nice for tea to take my mind off my shame.

A loud shout of 'Oi! You!' disturbed my thoughts. I looked over my shoulder in the direction of the call and saw two of the senior boys running towards me, waving their arms. It seemed clear to me that there was a good hiding in the making in this situation. I did not know why they were after me, but I did not intend to stay to find out. I sprinted off as fast as I could.

Even as I began my frantic dash in a bid to escape whatever my pursuers had in store for me, I knew that it was a forlorn effort. There was no way I could outstrip these two strongly built lads. I had seen them run in the school sports and had envied their fleetness of foot.

Nevertheless, like a poor hare on the coursing field, I had to make the attempt. Surrender was unthinkable.

I ran as though my life depended upon it, narrowly avoiding a horse-drawn coal cart as I swept round the corner of Wellington Street and knocking the shopping basket out of the hand of an old lady as she was putting the latch key in her front door. A bread deliveryman placing a loaf on a dirty doorstep in Gordon Street saw me coming and stood in the centre of the pavement, arms outstretched.

'Where do you think you are going?' he shouted. I ducked under his arm and kept running. My hunters followed my example.

Instead of making a straight run for Aunt Elsie's house, I tried to throw my pursuers off the track by going up a side street – but to no avail. The two boys were gaining on me all the time. Eventually, after what seemed a marathon run –

although it could have lasted only three or four minutes – I lost the will to survive. I stopped and leaned against a wall, panting for breath.

Within a few seconds the boys pounced on me. Taking an arm each, they began to drag me back in the direction of St Mary's.

'What's up?' I gasped. 'What have I done?'

'Running away from school,' said one of my captors, prodding me in the back with his knee to keep me moving.

'But it's going home time.' I said. 'I was going home for my tea.'

'It's not going home time,' said the other boy. 'It's only playtime. There's two more lessons yet. Mr Blyth'll kill you.'

The full horror of my situation dawned on me. Running away from school was the major crime. There was no other offence to compare with it. I began to snivel.

'It's no good you roaring,' said the first boy. 'You're for it when we get back to school. Serves you right and all.'

Playtime had just finished as I was marched through the school gates. There was an odd silence as 150 pupils waited to see how my crime would be punished.

Mr Blyth stood at the bottom of the steps leading up to the junior section. He had his hands in his pockets and he was swaying backwards and forwards. Even in my moment of terror I could see that he was enjoying the situation. I was led towards him like a human sacrifice.

'We caught him all right, Sir,' said one of the boys. He had every cause to feel pleased with himself and he was making the most of his moment of glory.

'So I see,' said Mr Blyth. He stared at me for several seconds. I was still snivelling and would have liked to wipe my nose, but my captors still had a firm grip on my arms.

Eventually Mr Blyth spoke. 'You know what you've done, don't you?'

'No, Sir.'

'Yes you do. But I'll tell you all the same. You left the precincts during school hours without permission from the headmaster or a member of his staff.'

He made it sound as though I had masterminded a mass break-out from Alcatraz.

'I didn't mean to, Sir,' I said, in a half-hearted attempt to come up with some form of defence.

'Of course you meant to,' said Mr Blyth, rapidly losing his patience. 'You absconded. That's what you did. You absconded.'

'Did I, Sir?'

'Yes, you did, lad. Do you know what abscond means?'

'No, Sir.'

'Then I'll tell you. It means to leave furtively. In other words, you were trying to sneak off. This is a very serious business. What do you think would happen if every boy and girl at this school did what you just did?'

'I don't know, Sir.'

'We would have an empty school, wouldn't we? And if the school was empty, all the teachers would be out of work, including me. I wouldn't like that very much.'

Mr Blyth smiled and looked around the assembled pupils to signal that he had made a joke. Dutifully, everybody roared with laughter.

'Right,' said the deputy head, tiring of the verbal tormenting. 'You will stop in after school tonight to make up for your absence this afternoon. Report to me as soon as the bell goes.'

At the end of lessons I went to Mr Blyth and, as everyone else trooped home, I began my detention. Sitting alone in the classroom was not an ordeal. In fact, it made a pleasant change to have a little elbow room and to be free of the jostling, fidgeting mass encountered on all sides during lessons.

But the novelty soon wore off. After about 15 minutes I grew

109

tired of rummaging around among the contents of my desk and decided to read the four pages from an old copy of the boys' paper, the *Wizard*, that I had folded up small and hidden in the torn lining of my jacket. I had put the pages there for just such an emergency – to combat the emotion that all schoolboys feared most: boredom.

I read the stories twice and studied the jokes so intently that the comicalities no longer seemed funny. Carefully returning the pages to my pocket lining, I crept to the door and peered out in the hope that I could see the assembly hall clock, the only public timepiece in the building.

Unfortunately, from that angle it was hidden by a tall cabinet, and as I dare not step outside the door in case Mr Blyth saw me, I had to content myself with the thought that I could not possibly be detained for much longer.

There was not a sound in the building. It appeared completely deserted, but I assumed that Mr Waterson and Mr Blyth were sitting in their little office at the end of the hall, smoking their pipes and discussing the day's activities.

I consoled myself with the knowledge that when they went home, I would be set free. I just hoped that they did not have too much to talk about that night.

Returning to my seat, I let my imagination run riot and pretended that I was Ronald Colman in the film *The Prisoner of Zenda*, playing the king who was locked up by the dashing but evil Rupert.

Soon I became tired of all this mental activity and, resting my head on my folded arms as they lay on the desk lid, I fell asleep.

A screaming voice brought me back to reality. It was shouting 'Ronnie!' and, although it seemed to be coming from far away, it awoke me with such a start that I kicked over the desk. The contents of the ink well went all over my face and the floor.

Not used to waking in such alien surroundings, it took me a

few seconds to remember where I was and what I was doing there. Another screech of 'Ronnie!' sent me scurrying to the window.

Looking out, I saw my mother standing alone in the middle of the playground. She was wearing her grey coat with the imitation fur round the hem and a matching cloche hat that she thought made her look like the film actress, Irene Dunne.

She was waving her handbag round her head as if she vas standing in a huge crowd and trying to draw attention to herself. Agitation was reflected in every sound she uttered, every move she made.

'Ronnie!'

I pushed open the window and shouted, 'I'm up here, Mam!'

My mother took a step back. A look of relief crossed her face, soon to be replaced by one of thunderous anger.

'What are you doing up there, Ronnie?'

'I've been kept in after school.'

'Kept in after school!' she howled. 'Do you know what time it is? It's gone seven o'clock. I've been worried to death about you.'

'Sorry, mam, it wasn't my fault, honest.'

My mother's shrill cries had carried like a siren on the quiet evening air and they brought the school caretaker, Mr Walpole, running from his house outside the school gates. He rushed over to my mother, who was still standing in the centre of the playground.

'What's up, missus? What's going on? What's all the noise for?' he asked. Mr Walpole, known to the school wags as Mr Tadpole, was a nervous man. It was said that he remained shell-shocked from his experiences in the Great War, and his unexpected encounter with my furious mother could have done little to help his recovery.

'What's up?' echoed my mother. 'I'll tell you what's up. They've got my Ronnie locked up in there, that's all.'

She made it sound as though I was tied up in a padded cell, being detained during His Majesty's Pleasure.

'And look at his face,' she continued, pointing up to the ink stains round my eyes. 'They've been beating him up. His face is covered in bruises. He's black and blue.'

'No they haven't, mam. It's only ink,' I shouted, but it was plain to see she preferred the worst possible interpretation.

Mr Walpole was becoming as agitated as my mother, hopping from one foot to the other and keeping a wary eye on her handbag as it swung perilously near his head.

'You'll have to make less noise, missus. You're disturbing half the street,' he said. 'Just shut up a minute and I'll fetch the key and let him out. They must have forgotten he was still in there.'

'I should think so, too,' said my mother, only slightly placated. 'I don't know what the world's coming to, locking up kids on their own for half the night.' Exaggeration came freely to her when she was worried or frightened.

My release from captivity was effected smoothly and simply and my mother led me back to Aunt Elsie's house without another word. But I knew from experience that she was thinking a lot.

I also knew that the incident would be the talk of the St Mary's neighbourhood and that the following day's return to school would not be free of trouble.

And so it turned out – with the threat of expulsion in the air and Aunt Elsie emerging as the most unlikely, not to say dubious, peacemaker in the history of pupil–teacher–parent relationships.

Aunt Elsie was a willing listener when my mother told her of my detention, probably because she had been roped in to help in the search for me and resented having her evening ruined by the frantic goings-on that would have been generated by her excitable sister.

112

'I'd have it out with them at that school if I were you, our Madge,' she said.

'Don't you worry,' said my mother. 'They're going to feel the sharp end of my tongue, I can tell you.'

Uncle Ted, who was a confirmed pacifist, despite the contrary evidence of his two massive cauliflower ears, had been listening to all this while cleaning the saucepans in the kitchen.

He popped his head round the door and said, 'I don't know what all the fuss is about. We were always being kept in late when I was at school. It happened all the time.'

Aunt Elsie flared. 'It's nothing to do with you, Ted. You just get on with those pans.'

As instructed, Ted resumed his chores in the kitchen. Like all the husbands of the Perkins women, he knew his place in the order of things.

Even though it meant losing time off work, my mother escorted me to school the following morning, her resolve to vent her anger on someone in authority undiminished by a night's sleep.

One or two of the early-arriving pupils seemed well aware that a confrontation of some sort was on the cards. They knew that parents seldom came into the school building unless they intended to have a row with a teacher or attend the Christmas concert.

As my mother marched up the stairs to the first floor, we were followed, Pied Piper fashion, by about a dozen boys and girls, all eager to see the showdown.

We entered the assembly hall and my mother spotted Mr Blyth standing by the door leading into classroom 2b. Mr Blyth knew what was coming, because he was just finishing a conversation with Mr Walpole, who was looking even more edgy than usual.

My mother wasted no time with opening pleasantries. 'What happened to my Ronnie last night?' she demanded.

Mr Blyth spread his arms airily, obviously having made up his mind to treat the whole business as lightly as possible.

'It was all a mistake, Mrs Bassett,' he said, smiling sweetly in the hope that it would dilute her wrath. 'I just went home and forgot that I had left him in the classroom. I'm ever so sorry, but it's easily done.'

The explanation did nothing to calm my mother. In fact, it had the opposite effect. She hardly reached up to Mr Blyth's shoulders, but she squared up to him like a pugilist, looking up into his face and spluttering with rage.

'That's the daftest thing I ever heard,' she yelled. 'Anything could have happened to the boy. There could have been an earthquake for a start.'

I could not follow my mother's line of argument with that last observation and it was plain that Mr Blyth did not understand it either.

Still beaming, he put his arm round my mother's shoulders and said, 'Now come on, Madge, calm down. Don't get so excited.'

'Don't tell me to calm down,' said my mother, shrugging off his arm and continuing to glare up at him.

Mr Blyth persisted. 'You must learn to take life easier, Madge, otherwise you will never get fat like me.'

I was beginning to wonder why he was calling my mother by her Christian name when she suddenly swung her arm and punched him in the face.

There was a burst of startled 'oohs!' and 'aahs!' from the pupils who had crowded into the assembly hall. It was all turning out to be far more exciting than they could possibly have hoped for.

My mother's thin, blue-veined fist bounced off Mr Blyth's jaw like a dried pea off the skin of a kettle drum. He threw back his head and laughed.

'You're a little demon, Madge,' he said. 'There's no doubt about it, you're a little demon.'

114

My mother stood her ground, fist raised and full of defiance. I felt both proud and ashamed of her at that moment.

There was a chance that the whole incident might have passed off without further development. Mr Blyth clearly regarded my mother's attempt at pugilism as a marvellous joke and might not have taken any further action.

Mr Waterson, the headmaster, was made of different stuff. Army life had taught him that striking a senior officer was an offence carrying almost unspeakable punishment. And Mr Waterson put schoolteachers into the senior officer category when compared with rank-and-file parents.

He marched across the assembly hall, waving pupils out of his way as he approached the scene of the crime.

'This will not do, Mrs Bassett,' he said in his sternest tones. 'I cannot allow you to inflict physical abuse on a member of my staff.'

'He started it,' said my mother, still warlike.

'No, he did not start it,' corrected Mr Waterson. 'You attacked Mr Blyth without cause or reason. I must warn you that I shall have to put this matter before the school managers. They may well decide to take out a summons against you.'

'A summons?' said my mother, frightened by the mere sound of the word. 'Being taken to court, do you mean?'

'That's exactly what I mean, Mrs Bassett. You can't go around hitting people just when you feel like it.'

To his eternal credit, Mr Blyth tried to intercede on my mother's behalf.

'She didn't hurt me, Mr Waterson,' he said. 'She only did it on the spur of the moment.'

'That's not the point, Mr Blyth,' said the headmaster, who was beginning to sound as though he was conducting the preliminary hearing of an army court martial. 'The fact remains that she struck you. In any case, some of the worst things in life are done on the spur of the moment. That's well worth remembering, Mr Blyth.'

115

All this talk of summonses and court cases conjured up a mental picture of my mother behind bars and launched me into an outburst of uncontrollable tears.

'Now look what you've done,' said my mother, pulling me towards her in a bear-like hug.

Ignoring my howls, Mr Waterson then delivered the most awful news of all.

'I am afraid you will have to take your son home until we decide what to do with him. I don't think we can keep him at this school any longer. He will have to go somewhere else. He's obviously a bad influence here. And so are you.'

Accepting defeat, my mother turned and strode off, pulling me with her. As she reached the door leading from the assembly hall, she shouted over her shoulder, 'I'll bet you wouldn't have done this if his father had been alive.'

I moped around Aunt Elsie's house all that day. The more I thought about our dilemma, the worse it seemed. The prospect of my mother going to prison was too terrible to contemplate. I had seen what happened to James Cagney at the pictures, and I could not see her coping with the problems he faced in those penitentiary dramas.

Almost as bad was the thought that I would have to go to a new school and mix with strangers in alien surroundings. The outlook appeared bleak.

After tea, a sombre affair with little conversation, Aunt Elsie instructed Uncle Ted to clean the brass ornaments that littered the mantelpiece. She always found him a job to do in the evenings and he never quibbled.

'Now, our Madge,' said Aunt Elsie, 'what are you going to do about that school?'

'Nothing I can do now,' said my mother. Her fighting spirit was spent.

'Why don't you go back and have another word with them?'

'No use. If it was just Billy Blyth, I reckon I could get him to forget all about it. In fact, I'm sure I could. Daft as tripe is that Billy Blyth. I was in the same class as him when we were kids. We used to call him Silly Billy Blyth. We used to think he was a bit simple. How he ever became a school-teacher I shall never know. He never struck me as being sharp enough.'

'He was sharp enough to train as a teacher,' said Uncle Ted, standing in the kitchen doorway and rubbing vigorously at a brass replica of a trumpeting elephant.

'They took anybody after the war,' said Aunt Elsie.

'What about Waterson?' asked Uncle Ted, revealing a surprising determination to stay in the conversation. 'Why don't you ask him to let it drop?'

'He won't budge,' said my mother. 'He's as hard as nails. Got no feelings at all.'

Uncle Ted laughed. 'Well, he's changed a lot then,' he said. 'During the war he was a bit of a handful, even if he was an officer. And he was a devil for the girls. If some of the old squaddies in this town knew what he got up to with their wives and girlfriends when he came home on leave, they would knock his teeth in. Even now. As for his missus, I dread to think what she would say if she knew what he was like in those days.'

At this point I glanced across the table at Aunt Elsie. There was an expression on her face I could not remember seeing there before. It was as though she was recalling things that had not entered her mind for years.

After a long silence she got up from the table and picked up her coat and hat, which were lying on the wooden cover of the sewing machine in the corner of the room.

'I'm going round to that headmaster's house to have a word with him about all this,' she said. 'You never know your luck – he might change his mind.'

She was gone for more than an hour, and when she returned

her cheeks were flushed and her eyes were bright. She looked years younger.

'What did he say?' asked my mother, puffing nervously on yet another Woodbine.

'He says you'll hear no more about it. And Ronnie can go back to school tomorrow,' said Aunt Elsie. There was a total absence of the triumphant tone she usually adopted when she had scored a success at anything.

Uncle Ted looked mildly surprised. He was still wearing his leather apron, his standard uniform for the many household duties that came his way.

'How did you manage to get him to change his mind?' he said. 'Did you used to know him then?'

'I met him a few times. Years ago,' said Aunt Elsie. Her manner was casual.

'What did you say to him?' persisted Uncle Ted.

'Not much,' said Aunt Elsie. Her voice was soft, almost gentle, but it changed to her familiar dictatorial style as she added, 'Still, it's all over now, Ted, so you can get back to cleaning those ornaments.'

I could see that Uncle Ted was puzzled and would have liked to ask more questions, but he had been too well trained on both the Western Front and the domestic front to delay carrying out an order from someone in authority. He returned to his labours with the tin of Brasso in the kitchen.

Aunt Elsie was smiling reflectively as she removed her coat and hat. My mother lit another Woodbine to compound her relief that the ordeal was over.

I was told to go to bed, and as I climbed the stairs I heard Aunt Elsie say to my mother 'Well, Madge, like our Maud always says, the ghosts of the past are bound to come back to haunt you – sooner or later.'

I had no idea what she meant by that, but for once in my life I did not want to know. I was drained, physically and mentally, after the trials of the past two days. But I was glowing in the knowledge that the following morning I would resume my rightful place in that earthly paradise, Class 2b at St Mary's.

THE DAY IT RAINED
CATS AND DOGS
– AND OTHER CREATURES

B EING THE PROUD owner of a pet – however humble its place in the animal kingdom – was a source of great joy for the average working-class boy growing up in the Thirties.

In a curious way, such a possession gave his life an extra meaning, enabling his inbuilt desire to cater for the welfare of dumb creatures to blossom.

This, in turn, took his mind off the less palatable aspects of his own spartan existence, encouraging a feeling of material wealth, however fleeting that might be.

Such pets spanned a wide range, from spiders and beetles kept in matchboxes to faithful dogs, usually mongrels, that would follow their owners to school and wait patiently outside the playground gates for the children to complete their morning or afternoon education stints.

Not all dogs were as faithful and trustworthy as these canine paragons. A friend of mine, Billy Marlow, had an unhappy experience with a dog that left him mentally scarred for life, physically scarred for two or three days, and put him off roast lamb for ever.

Walking home from a Sunday morning wander in the woods, he came across a gypsy caravan parked by the side of the road. The women of this mobile residence could be seen on nearby doorsteps, trying to sell pegs.

121

The male head of the fraternity was giving his horse a drink of water from a bucket. Spotting Billy, he called him over.

'Hey, sonny,' he said. 'How would you like a dog of your own?'

Billy was interested, but asked the obvious question.

'How much, mister?'

'Nothing, sonny,' said the gypsy with a sly smile. 'I'll give you it for nothing. What do you think of that?'

Billy said he liked the idea very much, so the gypsy went round to the back of the caravan and brought out a black and brown mongrel terrier with a piece of rope tied round its neck.

'There you are,' said the man. 'He's all yours. You can take him home.'

Unable to believe his luck, Billy took the end of the rope and led the docile animal back to his house. When he got there, he was due for another surprise. His mother and father said he could keep the dog, providing he took it for a walk every day. Billy accepted the terms gratefully.

The Marlows then gathered round the living room table for their Sunday dinner and Billy noted with pleasure that they were to have a small leg of roast lamb – his favourite meat.

He felt at peace with the world, especially as his newly-acquired pet appeared to have settled comfortably in its new home and was lying stretched out on some coconut matting in the adjoining kitchen.

The roast lamb, giving off an appetising aroma, rested on a large round plate in the middle of the table. But not for long. As Mr Marlow rose, knife in hand, to carve the joint, the dog got up, padded nonchalantly into the living room, put its front paws on the table, grasped the leg of lamb firmly between its strong jaws, and shot out the conveniently open back door. It was never seen again – and neither was the leg of lamb.

Smaller pets that were popular with the schoolboy fraternity were white mice, costing threepence, and tortoises priced at sixpence.

Unfortunately, the former had a habit of gnawing their way out of their primitive cages and joining their brown domestic brethren behind the skirting boards.

The outcome of such liaisons between the 'tame' and the 'wild' could sometimes be seen when a skewbald creature popped out of a hole and scurried across the linoleum on short-cut route to its nest. Hygiene-conscious parents did not take kindly to these natural developments and banned the possession of white mice.

Sadly, tortoises had a habit of disappearing within days of their purchase. Left to its own devices, a tortoise would amble off, no matter how well fenced the garden might be.

Even the old dodge of tying a piece of string to its leg and anchoring it to a tree did not work. Overnight, the tortoise, with Houdini-like skill, would slip free of its restrictions and vanish. Hundreds of these slow but purposeful animals took off in this way, leaving their erstwhile owners tearful and pet-less.

The odd part is that they seldom, if ever, turned up in a neighbour's garden. Where they went to was a frequent topic for discussion when playground pundits got together to discuss weighty matters. The more cynical amongst us took the view that pet shop owners used to sneak round in the night and steal back the tortoises, thus selling the same ones over and over again.

Some lucky youngsters – few and far between – were able to keep rabbits. They were easily identified because they spent most of their time wandering with sacks around the woods and fields, looking for dandelions, or scrounging discarded lettuce leaves from greengrocers.

Other boys had to be content with sharing a pet with their

parents. This usually took the form of a budgerigar. No matter how hard-up they might be in other directions, many families kept such a bird, usually housed in an ornate cage on a fancy silver-painted stand.

One or two boys in my class boasted that their budgerigars could talk fluently. They claimed that their vocabularies went far beyond 'who's a pretty boy, then?'

For instance, Ralph Bunnidge insisted that his bird could recite the nursery rhyme, 'Humpty Dumpty', backwards. No one believed him, of course, but it ranked high on our list of the best tall stories.

Bertie Tassell alleged that his parents' budgerigar knew every swear word in the English language, plus several German oaths, the latter being picked up from the boy's father, who had served with the British Army in Germany after World War One.

One day a gang of us challenged Bertie, demanding the chance to hear this foul-mouthed bird in full spate. We were intrigued by bad language and felt certain there must be many more swear words – and far worse – than those we had heard in our limited experience of life. Here, we thought, might be a golden opportunity to take a crash course in obscenities.

At a time when he knew that his mother and father would be out of the house, Bertie invited five of us round to listen to what he promised would be a flood of cursing.

Naturally enough, we were disappointed. We stood in a circle round the cage, faces pressed against the bars, willing the yellow-and-black-feathered bird to let rip. It ignored us completely and continued to peck at its chunk of cuttle-fish.

Cyril Braithwaite, braver than the rest of us, decided to risk eternal purgatory by speaking all the swear words he knew – in the hope that this would encourage the bird to reciprocate in kind. He said 'damn' and 'blast' and 'hell' and 'sod it', blushing crimson as he uttered the taboo words. It was a waste of time.

The budgerigar stopped eating its cuttle-fish and concentrated on looking at itself in its little mirror.

We left Bertie's house in disgust. As we marched off down the street, Bertie shouted after us, 'He'll start now you are going. I'll bet you.'

We chose to ignore him. He had had his chance to make his reputation – and so had his budgerigar. They had failed dismally, and therefore did not merit further consideration such was the stern code of schoolboys in those days.

Because of the nomadic life led by my mother and me during my early years, the range of pets available to me was strictly limited, depending entirely on the goodwill of the aunts and uncles who were providing the roof over our heads.

Like quite a few others, I found that the cheapest and most convenient pet to fit in with my restricted circumstances was the simple silkworm.

Easily obtained from the local pet shop for a few pence, they could be kept in a shoe box on the window sill of the outside lavatory, where they caused no problems for anyone. They could be fed on a few mulberry leaves and were delightful to watch, even though they never lived up to their owners' expectations.

My aim in life was to gather enough strands of 'silk' to make a handkerchief for my mother, although I did not have the slightest idea how I would achieve this manufacturing miracle.

As it turned out, the problem never arose, because the silkworms usually died within a few days and I had to wait until I had gathered two or three pennies in order to start the ambitious process all over again.

Some friends of mine kept goldfish. These were boys whose fathers were skilled at darts or table skittles and were able to win the fish when fairs visited the neighbourhood.

Regrettably, the goldfish seldom lasted long, probably due to the bizarre diet imposed upon them by their young, well-meaning owners, who did not know that little bits of cold Yorkshire pudding and the ends of ice cream cones were no substitute for ants' eggs.

Equally short-lived were the tiny chicks that street traders would hand out in exchange for a few items of secondhand clothing.

The chicks, a mere day or two old, would be taken indoors and placed in the ubiquitous shoe box near the fire to keep them warm.

The pleasure of watching these lovely little yellow balls of fluff hopping about and cheeping loudly was usually cancelled out the following morning when the young owner hurried from his or her bed only to find the tiny new pet lying dead in the corner of the shoe box.

For a long time, the nearest I got to having a genuine pet of my own – admittedly on a part-time basis – was through the kindness of Mrs Greenaway, who lived in a newly-built bungalow in what we council estate boys regarded as one of the posher parts of town.

I met her purely by chance during a violent rainstorm when I was helping Jimmy Meadows distribute the local evening newspaper. Jimmy was three or four years older than me and I was always envious of the fact that he was never without a few coppers to spend, part of the wages he received as a delivery boy for the newsagent in Albion Road.

Jimmy usually had a large bag of broken toffee in his pocket and it was the promise of an occasional dip into these caches of chewy delights that encouraged me to offer my services on his paper round.

The rain was lashing down the night I bumped into Mrs Greenaway. I was running as fast as I could in order to deliver the last paper in the batch that Jimmy had given me. It was a pointless exercise because I was already soaking wet. A few more minutes in the deluge would not have made much difference to my soggy state.

With my head down, I did not see Mrs Greenaway, umbrella raised, opening the gate to her front garden. The collision must have hurt her more than it did me, but she did not cry out or express anger at my careless behaviour. Instead she put her hands on my shoulders and looked at me closely.

'You poor lad,' she said. 'You are absolutely wet through. Come inside. We'll soon get you dried off.'

She led me into the cosy bungalow and took off my hat and coat, hanging them on the wire guard in front of the well-stacked coal fire. She made me a mug of Oxo and handed me a plate with four chocolate biscuits on it. 'You'll feel better when you have had these,' she said.

As we warmed ourselves in front of that cheering fire, we talked about my life at school and the many pleasures it gave me. At one stage I made her laugh and she responded by ruffling her hand through my hair and patting my cheek.

I noticed three framed photographs of children on the mantelpiece. Two were only toddlers and I could not tell whether they were boys or girls. The third was of a boy about my age.

Mrs Greenaway never made any reference to them and I did not ask who they were. Once, through what must have been a slip of the tongue, she called me Bobbie. At that moment her face took on a sad look, but she soon became her bright, smiling self again.

I could tell that she liked me, and I liked her, too, so when she said that I could call to see her whenever I was passing by I felt supremely happy. I knew I had found a true friend.

I visited her often in the weeks that followed and she always welcomed me with open arms. I can picture her now, standing on the doorstep and smiling with genuine pleasure at the sight of me.

127

Her hair was the colour of brandy snap and it was always tightly curled, living up to the popular term of the times, a permanent wave.

She wore neat, brightly coloured pinafores and must have had many of these garments, for I never saw her wearing the same one twice in succession.

Her husband was nice, too. He was the manager of a pork butcher's shop in the town centre, a marvellous food emporium rich with the aroma of black pudding, roast pork, ham and pork pies.

He was a heavy smoker, but, unlike many of the traders of the period, he never indulged his habit within the store. If he felt the need for tobacco he would leave his assistant in charge and go out onto the pavement, where he would draw with great relish on expensive Passing Cloud cigarettes taken from a bright pink packet.

Mr and Mrs Greenaway were very fond of each other. In the mornings, before he set off for work, they would kiss on the doorstep.

When he reached the garden gate he would turn, smile and salute her by tipping the rim of his trilby. She would watch him until he reached the end of the road, when he would turn again and wave.

Mrs Greenaway would then put down the empty milk bottle she was holding and pick up the full one from the little wooden container her husband had made for the purpose. I saw them carry out this daily ritual on several occasions and Jimmy Meadows, who also delivered morning papers, told me that this happy couple never deviated from the routine, come rain or shine.

Apart from the pleasure of Mrs Greenaway's company and the joy of receiving the little gifts with which she surprised me at regular intervals, there was the bonus of being allowed to take her little spaniel, Patsy, for walks.

128

I felt honoured to be trusted with this pedigree bitch and when I took her for walks through the woods that skirted the ironstone workings I liked to pretend that she was mine, and that I owned kennels full of champion dogs that always won the first prizes at Cruft's.

Mrs Greenaway reminded me often that I must never let Patsy off her lead and I tried to follow her instructions to the letter – except for the day when I met up with several boys from school and I unleashed her in the hope that she would prove to be a hunter and catch a wild rabbit.

As it happened, she just ran off into the densest part of the wood and it took me half an hour to catch her. I felt ashamed that I had let Mrs Greenaway down, but I did not have the courage to tell her what I had done.

I thoroughly enjoyed taking Patsy for her walks, especially as Mrs Greenaway gave me an iced cake when I returned her treasured pet safe and sound. Sometimes she would give me twopence and tell me to buy myself some sweets.

Whenever she did that I deeply regretted that I had let Patsy off her lead, but then I salved my conscience with the convenient thought that the little dog had been delighted to romp on her own and had not come to any harm during her spell of complete freedom.

So, apart from my short-lived silkworms and my strolls with Patsy, I hardly fell into the category of a major pet owner, a fact that did not go unnoticed among my contemporaries.

Then came the traumatic day when a succession of creatures passed through my hands with a speed that left its mark for weeks to come.

The day started quietly enough. I had decided to walk to uncle Harry's allotment to see if I could find any white butterflies on his cabbages. They made useful pets even though their lifespan seemed less than the silkworms.

I was walking along Carrington Street when the upstairs

window of number 39 shot up and Billy Compton popped out his head.

'Hey, Bassett,' he shouted. 'Do you want something for nothing?'

As an opening gambit it was irresistible, even though I knew that Billy, one of nature's born loners, was not noted at school for his generosity.

'What?' I said. 'What have you got?'

'Come up the entry and I'll show you,' said Billy. With that he slammed down the bedroom window and disappeared from view.

Still suspicious, I walked up the entry dividing the two terraced houses. Billy was waiting for me at the back gate. He let me in and led me to a kennel beside the outside lavatory.

'You can have one of these puppies if you like,' he said. He pointed inside the kennel, where I saw a doleful looking black bitch. Four fairly helpless puppies were snuffling around her, anxious to be fed.

'My dad's going to drown 'em when he comes home from work tonight,' said Billy. 'So I'm trying to give 'em away before he gets back.'

I knew all about Billy's dad. He was a big man who worked for the council and seemed to spend most of his time digging holes in the roads. He was far from squeamish when it came to disposing of people's unwanted animals, particularly litters of kittens and puppies, which he would dispatch with merciless efficiency in a large bucket of water.

We were all frightened of Mr Compton and steered well clear of any holes he happened to be working on. It seemed to us that it was only a small step from executing dumb animals to getting rid of small boys.

'Do you want one, then?' asked Billy.

I looked down at the little creatures and warmed to the prospect of owning a dog of my own.

'You can have two if you like,' said Billy.

130

I turned down this new offer. Getting Aunt Flo to accept one dog into the house would be a problem. The odds against two being acceptable were beyond calculation.

So I settled for the one, carefully putting my hand in the kennel and lifting out a tiny, whimpering creature. Its mother looked on passively. She must have had this experience several times before.

I thanked Billy for the gift and set off for Aunt Flo's house. Even before I got there, I knew I was doomed to be disappointed.

'No, Ronnie, sorry,' she said.

'I'll look after it properly,' I said, desperately trying to get her to change her mind. It was a waste of time.

'I'm sorry, my duck,' she said firmly, 'but it's out of the question. There's the mess and everything. And who would look after it while you are at school?'

Her argument was too strong to dispute. I knew she was right, but this did not lessen the disappointment. Uncle Bill sealed the matter when he observed, 'Poor little thing. It's far too young to have left its mother. You had better take it back.'

Cradling the puppy in both hands, I began the long walk back to Billy Compton's house, but I had not gone far when I had a brainwave. Lennie Cunliffe, the schoolboy entrepreneur and playground wheeler-dealer, came into my mind. If anybody could come up with an answer to the problem of saving the puppy, Lennie was the lad.

As usual, I found him in his father's shed, counting his cigarette cards. I told him about the fate that awaited the puppy if I returned it to the Compton family and asked for his help.

Lennie leaned back in the old deckchair that his father used to take a nap in when he became bored with gardening.

'Do you mean you want me to be your agent?' he asked.

'How do you mean – agent?' I asked in reply. 'I don't know what you mean.'

131

'Do you want me to act as your agent?' repeated Lennie, slowly and carefully, as though explaining a basic fact to a simpleton.

'Do you mean like an insurance agent?' I said.

'No, not really,' said Lennie wearily. 'My dad says that an agent is someone who looks after things for people. Helps them get things. Sorts things out for them.'

'That sounds all right,' I said, although I did not fully understand what he was talking about. 'Will you be my agent, then?'

'Course I will,' said Lennie.

There was a long silence. Lennie was deep in thought and I stood holding the puppy, which was beginning to look more fragile by the minute.

Eventually Lennie jumped out of the deckchair. 'I know what we'll do. We'll swap it for something else. And we'll swap it with someone we know will look after it.'

'Who can we swap with?' I asked, marvelling at Lennie's brain power.

'Well, it's obvious,' said Lennie triumphantly. 'Gordon Brown, of course!'

Of course. It had to be Gordon Brown. He lived on the other side of the town and was noted for the fact that he had more pets than any dozen schoolboys put together.

This was due to the example set by his father, who had a smallholding and was a devoted animal lover. Mr Brown's affection for all creatures, great and small, had rubbed off on the admirable Gordon.

We ran all the way to Mr Brown's place and were breathless when we arrived. Gordon was mixing some chickenfeed, one of his many duties on the smallholding.

He looked at us somewhat suspiciously. I got the impression that he had had dealings with Lennie in the past and was wondering what his visitor had up his sleeve on this occasion.

'Ronnie's got a dog to swap. Haven't you, Ronnie?' said Lennie, refusing to waste time with any preliminaries to a possible deal.

'What sort of dog?' asked Gordon. Even his uncertainty about Lennie's trustworthiness could not dampen his enthusiasm for an exciting swapping session.

'Show him it, Ronnie,' said my self-appointed agent.

I reached inside my coat and brought out the shivering puppy. I could feel its heart beating fast as I held it up.

Gordon looked long and hard at the subject of the potential transaction.

'What breed is it?' he asked.

'It's a Great Dane,' said Lennie, choosing to overlook the fact that the puppy obviously came from a long line of mongrel terriers.

'Doesn't look much like a Great Dane to me,' said Gordon. 'It's not big enough, for a start.'

'Well, to be honest,' said Lennie, 'it's what is called a Small Dane. It's the same make, though. Isn't it, Ronnie?'

'Yes,' I said. Lying came easily when you were in partnership with Lennie Cunliffe.

'Never heard of a Small Dane,' said Gordon. 'There's no such animal.'

'Oh yes there is,' insisted Lennie. 'Ronnie's got a fag card at home with a picture of one of them on it. That's right isn't it, Ronnie?'

'Yes, that's right,' I confirmed. The lies were beginning to flow like tap water.

It was plain that Gordon had more faith in me than he had in Lennie. I was flattered, but at the same time ashamed of my duplicity.

'Tell you what, then,' said Gordon. 'I'll give you one of these baby rabbits for it.'

He pointed at one of a line of hutches. It contained four or

133

five little black-and-white rabbits, huddled in one of the corners.

An experienced campaigner in the world of schoolboy deals, Lennie refused to show any enthusiasm for the offer. He whistled through the wide gap in his front teeth and shook his head disdainfully.

'No,' he said. 'A puppy, especially a Small Dane, is worth far more than a rabbit. They're two a penny they are. We want something better than that.'

'Well, I haven't got anything else to swap,' said Gordon, showing all the signs of being a worthy adversary for the cunning Lennie. 'Take it or leave it. I don't care.'

'All right, then,' said Lennie. 'Tell you what. Give us one of your pigeons *and* the rabbit. That seems fair to me.'

Gordon mustered a hollow laugh to show his contempt for such an outlandish suggestion. He jerked his thumb in the direction of the shed containing his birds.

'They are all champions in there,' he said. 'They would fly round the world and back if I wanted them to. They're worth millions. My dad says so.'

Never afraid to take brinkmanship to the very edge, Lennie turned as if to leave.

'Come on, Ronnie,' he said. 'It's a waste of time talking to him. He doesn't know a good deal when he sees one.'

I began to follow Lennie along the path leading out of the smallholding, feeling that we were the losers in this particular encounter, but I had under-estimated my agent's talents. Gordon ran after us and began tugging at Lennie's sleeve.

'Okay, then, you can have a pigeon as well,' he said, 'but it won't be one of my best ones. I'll give you a stray one that flew into the loft with my other birds yesterday.'

'Let's have a look at it,' said Lennie.

We went into the shed and Gordon pointed to a rather dowdy bird perched on its own. It lacked the perkiness and sheen

of its companions and appeared out of place in these surroundings.

'That's it,' said Gordon. 'You can have that one.'

'It doesn't look much,' said Lennie. 'Can it fly?'

'Course it can fly,' said Gordon. 'How do you think it got
here in the first place?'

'Right, then,' said Lennie, 'we'll have it. But we want to pick
our own rabbit. You are not going to palm us off with the worst
one in the litter.'

Somewhat reluctantly, Gordon agreed, and we went back to
the rabbit hutch to make our selection.

Gordon fetched a small cardboard box from the outhouse
that served as his father's workshop and gently placed our
choice in it. For good measure, he dropped in a dandelion leaf.
Gordon was the most considerate of animal lovers.

He then asked the most important question. 'How are you
going to take the pigeon home? You'll have to hang on to it
because if it gets away you'll never see it again. Strays are like
that. You'll have to keep it in the same place for days and feed it
well, otherwise it will never come back when you let it out for a
fly round. That's why they're called homing pigeons. If they
don't know which is their home they wander off.'

'Lend us that,' said Lennie, pointing to an old, rusty bird cage
balanced on a pile of rubbish at the back of the shed. 'You'll
bring it back, won't you, Ronnie?'

Gordon did not appear too keen on the idea, but he went
along with it. The scrawny pigeon was put into the cage without
too much fuss or loss of feathers and Lennie and I set off in the
direction of Aunt Flo's house.

Halfway along Shaftesbury Street, Lennie put the cage on the
pavement and said, 'What are you going to pay me for doing the
deal?' The entrepreneurial spirit burned brightly in Lennie's
breast.

'I didn't know I had to pay you,' I said, naïve to the end. I ought to have remembered that Lennie Cunliffe never did anything for nothing.

'It's what my dad calls a commission,' he said.

'I haven't got any money,' I replied.

'Have you got any fag cards?'

As luck would have it, I had about 50 that I had won playing skimmers and floaters in the school playground a couple of days earlier. I put down the cardboard box and searched through my pockets for the cards, which I duly handed to Lennie.

'They'll do,' he said, and with that he turned and strode off, leaving me to struggle back to Ivy Street with the bird cage in one hand and the cardboard box under my other arm.

As I walked along I thought desperately of ways in which I could house my two new pets – always assuming that Aunt Flo and Uncle Bill would let me keep them.

I felt sure that Uncle Bill would knock together a small hutch for my rabbit, but how would I house the pigeon? Like many of the events in my young life, I had not thought it through properly.

Suddenly I had the answer – Norman Mason's hen coop, the one in which his mother planned to keep pullets once she could afford to buy them.

Norman, as previously recorded, was my best friend. I was sure he would let me keep the pigeon in the coop until I could find permanent accommodation for it. And as Norman's back garden faced on to Aunt Flo's back garden, I would be in close contact with my new pet. My problems were over.

I had not felt so cheerful for ages. To have one pet was a joy; to own two was beyond my wildest dreams. Unfortunately I had not reckoned on Frank Pearson appearing on the scene.

Frank was in my class at school and just lately he had become very friendly with Norman. To be honest, I was a little jealous of the liaison, experiencing the truth of the old saying that two's company, three's a crowd.

Frank had red hair and many freckles, and was tall for his years. He always looked smart. His trousers were never without a crease and his socks, straight and uncrumpled, were held up with strong white elastic.

He seldom seemed to get gravel rash on his kneecaps like the rest of us and he looked so neat he could have passed as one of the plaster models in the children's section of the Fifty Shilling Tailors.

Yet for all these failings, there was nothing namby-pamby about Frank Pearson. He was tough and assertive and had an answer for everything. He had the makings of a lawyer, both barrack room and courtroom. I was soon to be given a demonstration of these attributes.

I opened the little metal gate that led to the back door of Aunt Flo's council house and immediately spotted Norman and Frank leaning on the strands of wire that served as a dividing line between the tenants' gardens.

As usual, Frank looked well-scrubbed and as fit as a fiddle. Thinking back, I cannot recall him ever suffering from a cold, or even a runny nose for that matter. The clean handkerchief tucked into the top pocket of his jacket bore testimony to this not particularly enviable record.

'What have you got there, Ronnie?' asked Norman, eyeing with interest the cardboard box and the bird cage.

When I told them about my good fortune, Norman was quick with the vital question. 'Where are you going to keep them?'

'I'm going to ask my Uncle Bill to make me a hutch for the rabbit,' I said, 'and I was wondering if you would let me keep my pigeon in your mum's hen coop.'

'Course you can,' said Norman, as generous-hearted as ever. Frank Pearson had other ideas.

'Hang on a minute,' he said. 'You can't expect Norman to let you use his property for nothing. The council wouldn't allow it.'

I could not see what the council had to do with it, but my debating skills were not powerful enough to risk a challenge against Frank. I just wished I had Lennie Cunliffe with me to act as my agent in this tricky situation.

'I reckon,' said Frank, well aware that he was in command, 'that you ought to give Norman that rabbit in exchange for the use of his mam's hen coop for your pigeon.'

I looked at Norman, hoping he would reject the suggestion, but I was disappointed. The thought of gaining a rabbit at no cost to himself was too much for Norman. When it came to the ownership of pets, friendship had a habit of flying out the window.

The prospect of losing the rabbit before I had become used to the luxury of owning it was hard to take, but I consoled myself with the thought that at least I had a home for my pigeon.

And so the deal was struck. With considerable care we removed the pigeon from its cage and put it in the hen coop, making sure that the door latch was firmly placed.

All three of us were well aware that a fair amount of seed and monkey nuts would have to be fed to this tatty bird before we dare put its homing instincts to the test.

Norman and Frank went indoors with the rabbit, presumably to show the newly-acquired pet to Norman's mother, a jolly little lady who was very tolerant about such things.

I was left to gaze through the wire mesh of the hen coop and ponder on the problem of where I was going to find the money to pay for the pigeon's upkeep.

I had been standing there, deep in thought, for about five minutes when Mrs Mason's back door opened and out trooped Norman and Frank. Both looked glum, with Norman clearly on the verge of tears.

I was not too bothered about their apparent distress. What did concern me was the fact that Norman was holding the rabbit by its ears, with its limp body held out at arm's length in front of him.

'You should never hold a rabbit by its ears,' I said. 'It's cruel, and what's more, it addles their brains.'

'No need to worry about that,' said Frank, recovering his composure. 'It's dead.'

'Dead?' I echoed. 'But you've only had it five minutes. How can it be dead?'

Tears rolled down Norman's cheeks as he told the story. It appears that they took the rabbit into the living room, where it was given a friendly welcome by Mrs Mason, who was fond of animals.

Unhappily, the rabbit did not receive such a warm welcome from Mrs Mason's much-pampered ginger cat, Precious. No sooner had Norman put the rabbit on the dining table so they could take a closer look at it, than Precious, who had been sitting on the window sill, took a mighty leap across the room, landed on the table and killed the rabbit with one swift bite to the neck. It was all over in a few seconds.

We stood in silence for a while after Norman had completed his description of the scene of carnage. Out of the corner of my eye I could see Precious watching us from the kitchen window. I hated all cats at that moment.

And then the next disaster happened. We heard a creaking noise and turned to see the door of Mrs Mason's hen coop slowly swing open.

The three of us stood transfixed as my pigeon, which had been pecking about on the floor of the coop, strutted out into the garden, thrusting its scraggy neck in and out and cocking an eye in our direction as it did so.

'Don't move,' whispered Frank. 'If we frighten it, it will start to fly.'

The pigeon did not wait to be frightened. It soared into the air and landed on the guttering above Mrs Mason's spare bedroom.

I watched with a sinking heart as my bird jerked its head from side to side, obviously pondering on which direction to take. We gazed up at it helplessly, knowing full well that there was no way in which we could recover it. After what seemed an eternity, the pigeon flapped its wings vigorously and took to the skies, never to be seen again.

I was too upset to stay to watch the burial of the rabbit, which, I was told later, was interred with some ceremony next to the remains of Norman's recently-demised goldfish, also a victim of the murderously-inclined Precious.

Sitting in Aunt Flo's kitchen, I tried to take my mind off things by reading my newly-arrived *Chips* and *Funny Wonder* comics, which Uncle Bill bought for me every week.

It was difficult to accept the fact that, including the puppy I had swapped, I had lost three pets in little more than an hour.

Unable to settle down, I decided to call on Mrs Greenaway. I felt in need of the sight of a kindly face and the sound of a sympathetic voice.

What's more, there was just the chance that she would let me take Patsy for a walk. That might ease the pain.

Mrs Greenaway smiled when she opened her front door and saw me standing on the step.

'Hello, Ronnie,' she said. 'We haven't seen you for ages. Where have you been?'

'Nowhere, Mrs Greenaway,' I replied. 'I was just wondering if I could take Patsy for a walk.'

'Ah,' said Mrs Greenaway, a curious expression crossing her gentle face. 'Now that is not possible just at the moment. Come with me. I've got something to show you.'

She motioned me to wipe my shoes on the doormat and ushered me through the neatly-furnished bungalow and out into the equally neatly-planted back garden. We walked along the crazy paving path to Mr Greenaway's creosote-coated shed and she opened the door.

'Look in there, Ronnie,' she said.

I peeped in and saw Patsy curled up in a large blanket-lined basket. Huddled close to her were four puppies.

'She had them two days ago,' said Mrs Greenaway. 'There were five, but one of them died.'

As I stood there, looking down at Patsy and her puppies, I sensed that Mrs Greenaway was studying me closely.

'Ronnie,' she said, 'are you sure that you never let Patsy off her lead when you took her for walks?'

'No, Mrs Greenaway,' I said. 'Never.'

She patted my head affectionately. 'No, I'm sure you didn't,' she said, looking towards the bottom of the garden and adding, 'There must be a gap under the fence down there somewhere.'

I had not the faintest idea what she meant by that last observation. It was just another of the many remarks by grown-ups that meant absolutely nothing to me.

'Now, I've got some good news for you, Ronnie,' she continued. 'Three of the puppies have been spoken for, but as you have been such a good boy, taking Patsy for walks, Mr Greenaway and I have decided that you can have the fourth one. Would you like that?'

'Yes, please, Mrs Greenaway,' I said, 'but I don't think my Aunt Flo will let me keep it at her house.'

'Well, you must ask her,' said Mrs Greenaway. 'Even if she says no, when the time comes you can still have the puppy and give it to one of your little friends. How would that be?'

'That would be lovely, Mrs Greenaway,' I said, my mind working overtime on the possibilities arising from this most welcome gift.

As she conducted me back through the house, Mrs Greenaway paused by the glass cabinet that occupied pride of place in the front room.

'I nearly forgot,' she said. 'Mr Greenaway has left you those cigarette cards he promised to collect for you.'

141

She opened the cabinet and took out a pack of cards depicting popular garden flowers. They were in perfect condition.

Unlike some grown-ups, Mr Greenaway did not stuff the cards in his top pocket, thereby bending them at the corners or creasing them across the middle. He treated them as though they were fine pieces of bone china and would never dream of damaging them in any way.

I counted them hurriedly as Mrs Greenaway watched me with an indulgent smile. I thanked her and left as fast as I could. Even before I had carefully clicked shut the front garden gate, I knew exactly what I intended to do.

After all, there came a time in every small boy's life when the services of a good agent at the peak of his negotiating powers were far more valuable than 37 cigarette cards, even though they were in pristine condition.

Light of heart once more, I set off in the direction of Lennie Cunliffe's house.

CIGARETTE CARDS AND
A DREAM COME TRUE

WHEN I ARRIVED, Lennie was out, so I had to make my way home. My thoughts were in over-drive about 'agent' and commission. I desperately wanted the puppy, but I knew in my heart of hearts that there was no chance of me having it at the lodgings with my aunt. I would have to seek out Lennie's help at the very first opportunity – he was my only chance of being able to have the puppy. I'd take up his offer of being my 'agent' again; but agents, as Lennie had told me, had to be paid.

My childish plan was that I would ask Lennie to keep the puppy for me, perhaps in his shed. Of course, it didn't cross my mind that his parents' permission had to be sought. How was I going to pay Lennie to keep the puppy? Could I get a job at the butchers where Mr Greenaway was manager, as a delivery boy on Saturday mornings? That would be ideal, because I could get bones and scraps from the butchers.

My imagination was once again racing away. Realistically, though, the only thing I had of any value to me and to Lennie was my cigarette card collection, together with the 37 that Mrs Greenaway had given me. Lennie might be persuaded to look after the puppy if I gave him the cards, but when they ran out, what then? There was still the food. I could save some of my food at home and secrete any scraps that were about. I would save all the money that aunts and uncles gave me. I could wait utside the corner shop and when men came out with their cigarettes I'd ask them for the cards.

There was also Grandma Bassett. Perhaps I should let her into my secret. She was always willing to help me with whatever predicament I found myself in. I would call the dog 'Rex'. Taking him for walks would be not problem, as there was plenty of time between coming out of school and my mother getting home from the factory. I was getting quite excited at the prospect, thinking it was now within my reach to have what I had always wanted – a dog. A dog is like a real mate. You can play football with a dog, go for walks in the woods and by the river, throw sticks in the river so that the dog can get the stick and bring it back to you. There are endless possibilities.

However, when I arrived home, I was in for a surprise. My mother and Ray were in the front room waiting for me. As soon as I got in, my mother told me to sit down as she had something nice to tell me. She began by asking, 'How would you like a new dad?' I must have looked a bit puzzled, as she went on to explain that she and Ray were to be married in four weeks' time. I knew Ray liked my mother very much because he was always putting his arm around her, and there was the time at the Silver Jubilee event when he blew her a kiss and she blew him two back.

Ray came in then, telling me that we would move into a new house with a bathroom and a garden. It would be on a new council estate near to my friends, too. How wonderful, I thought. I would be like my friends, living in a house with a garden, and as well as my mother I'd have the much longed-for dad. Ray asked me how I felt about it all. I said I was happy about it, and then, quite without thinking, I said, 'Can I have a dog when we move to the house?' Unbeknown me, of course, this was the ideal time to ask for something like this. My mother and Ray were anxious to start off their married life without any problems, and, of course, Ray hitting it off with me was a major bonus. They obviously thought letting me have a pet would help enormously – which of course it did. What they didn't know was that I already had the puppy earmarked at Mrs Greenaway's house. However, when I explained about Patsy and the puppies, they both agreed that I would be able to have the puppy as soon as Mrs Greenaway said it could leave its mother.

I went to my room then, as I had a lot of thinking to do. Ray would now become part of my life. I would have a real dad and, what's more, when my friends started talking about things their dads could do, I could tell them that my dad had lived in Canada. He'd know all about the Mounted Police and the Rockies and all sorts of exciting things. What tales I could tell my friends.

My mother and Ray got married as planned. All the aunts and uncles attended the wedding, the aunts dressed up in hats and the uncles in their best suits with highly polished shoes. After the wedding we had a special tea at Aunt Flo's, with a large iced wedding cake and port and lemon for the aunts and beer for the uncles.

My mother, Ray and me moved into the new house. To me it was like moving into a palace. I even had a room of my own. I was soon able to have the puppy, which I called Rex, and life seemed just about perfect. My friend Norman and I took Rex for long walks in the woods and I was kept busy training him to do all sorts of things. My mother continued to work at the boot and shoe factory and Ray worked at the furnaces.

Several months after they were married, in the late summer of that year, my mother had yet another surprise for me. She told me that in a few months' time I would be having a brother or sister – she was expecting a baby. I asked her when it would be, not knowing too much about babies and how everything happened. This kind of thing was not discussed, as it was a simple case of children being seen and not heard in those days. Anyway, she told me it would be near to Christmas. So life went on in the household more or less as normal. My mother did seem to be sick quite often, but she still went to work. I wondered when it would all happen.

Then one morning I awoke and was aware of a terrific commotion going on in the house. My mother was still in bed, and my dad was rushing around the house doing things, even though he had only just finished the night shift at the furnace. I was quite worried about my mother, as she seemed to be in pain and distress. I didn't really want to go to school.

However, I soon changed my mind about that when a huge nurse appeared through the back door, carrying a large black bag and saying to my dad, 'I want hot water, and plenty of it.' I dodged quickly out of the way as she proceeded upstairs to my mother. My dad said I should get off to school and maybe when I arrived home there would be a nice surprise for me.

All day at school I was wondering what was going on at home. When the time came to go home, I ran all the way. As soon as I opened the back door I could hear the sound of a baby crying. I raced upstairs. My mother and Ray were both in the bedroom, and happily the nurse had gone. My mother said, 'You've got a baby sister, Ronnie.' I looked at this tiny little creature. A sister – I didn't know much about sisters, except my mother's sisters. But this was different – this was my very own sister. I would have to look after her. I knew that bullies at school often found the girls easy targets. I would never let anything happen to her.

Ray said my mother needed some rest, so I decided to take Rex for a walk. I had a lot of thinking to do. I was thinking how my dreams were all coming true together. My champion was now my dad, I had my pet dog and now a sister. All this seemed to point to a rosier future for me and my family. But would it be? I was still a child of the Thirties.